FLOATING THROUGH HOLLAND (AND BELGIUM)

Self-published by
Brenda Davison
through www.lulu.com

ISBN: 978-1-4092-0162-5

Copies can be ordered via the Internet
www.brenda-davison.org.uk
and follow the link to My Writing/Speaking

(Information about using the French canals can also
be found on this site).

or from www.lulu.com

or by telephoning the author
+44 (0)151 334 3805
or +44 (0)771 8351066

Floating Through Holland

(and Belgium)

by

Brenda Davison

Our new boat *Liberty*

Dedicated to my mother,
who would have loved to have shared
these adventures with us

BOOKS BY THE SAME AUTHOR

Floating Through France (2001) Librario Publishing Ltd.
ISBN 1-904440-19-3
What's All This About Stress? (1999) Tudor Business
Publishing Ltd. ISBN 1 872807 33 X
Stress Management for Teachers (1999) workbook and
audio-tape, Primary Teaching Services Ltd.
Preston.

About the author

Brenda thought she was a confirmed landlubber until she took up sailing at the age of 49 when she met the man who is now her second husband, John. He had his own boat and had been an enthusiastic sailor all his adult life. He was keen that she should enjoy sailing but said that he would give it up and sell his boat if she did not enjoy it. Thus presented with a challenge Brenda joined him on a flotilla holiday in the Mediterranean and from that moment she was 'hooked'.

They bought a 10.5 metre (35ft) catamaran, *Chefren*, which they eventually sailed out to Greece via the French canals and down the Italian coast. They were beguiled by the delights of France and four years later they returned to the French canals and bought *Liberty*, a steel canal cruiser. They now spend all their summers exploring the inland waterways of France.

Never a one to do things by halves Brenda gained her Yachtmaster's International Certificate of Competence with endorsement for the inland waterways (ICC & CEVNI). Being nervous of water she also took swimming lessons and learned to snorkel so as to more fully enjoy the pleasure of boating in warmer waters.

They live on the Wirral peninsula, Merseyside, and when they are not sailing Brenda also does some free-lance journalism.

The story of their first journey through the French canals *Floating Through France* was published in 2002.

Contents

List of Illustrations

SKETCH MAP OF HOLLAND
showing route with Liberty

Kampen

Harderwijk
Nulde
Deventer

Amsterdam

RHINE   Arnhem

HOLLAND

MAAS

GERMANY

BELGIUM   Maastricht

MEUSE

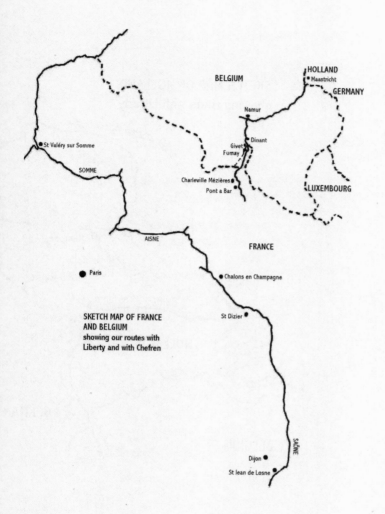

HOLLAND

BELGIUM

GERMANY

Maastricht

Namur

Dinant

Givet
Fumay

Charleville Mézières

Pont a Bar

LUXEMBOURG

St Valéry sur Somme

SOMME

AISNE

FRANCE

Paris

Chalons en Champagne

SKETCH MAP OF FRANCE
AND BELGIUM
showing our routes with
Liberty and with Chefren

St Dizier

SAÔNE

Dijon

St Jean de Losne

CHAPTER 1 – *Liberty*

Nervous.

The rain was relentless; it drummed on the cabin roof, ran down the windows of our boat and pooled on the side decks. The marina buildings were a grey blur seen through a fine curtain. The Dutch countryside across the waterway had disappeared behind a grey mist. We could have been perched on the edge of the world. John and I were huddled inside our new canal cruiser, *Liberty*, with our little diesel heater giving off a comforting warmth, and wondering when the rain was going to stop.

We had come to Holland six days previously to take possession of our new boat, *Liberty*. She was a 10.5 metre (35 ft), steel canal cruiser, built in the Netherlands in 1975 and we were here to begin a journey which would take us through Holland, around the edge of Belgium and finally into France where we were planning to find a boatyard where we could keep her during the winters.

John and I were second-time-arounders having both been married before. We had been cruising in Greece in a 10.5 metre sailing catamaran for the last few years realising a dream conceived when we married nearly 20 years previously. We had taken a short cut to Greece through the French canals and had such an interesting and eventful time that we told ourselves that one day we would come back and explore the rest of France by water. That 'one day' had now arrived.

When I first met John I had never sailed before, and did not think that I would ever want to do so. It is amazing what love can do. Not only did I learn to sail but I conquered a fear of water to develop a passion for this water-borne life that has now given us both a wonderful hobby and an interesting life-style I often think we are like Ratty and Moley in Wind in the Willows. I am Moley, once absorbed in domesticity but perhaps looking for a challenge. John is the water-rat who introduced me to the delights of 'messing about in boats'. And like Moley I had discovered that for me there is nothing better.

We now spend our summer months aboard our boat *Liberty* which will now be on the continental waterways. We had sailed to Greece, largely on our own, which had involved sailing overnight on some occasions and navigating from port to port. During this time we became very confident in handling the catamaran.

But now it was a different story. If I was absolutely honest I would have admitted that I was quite grateful to the rain which delayed the start of our journey from Holland. We had not had a motor cruiser before and we were not sure how she would handle. Not only that but we were in a new country, in a new boat and the charts were all in Dutch. We would need to pass through lots of locks, some of them would be big enough to accommodate huge sea-going boats, and through bridges which we might need to have lifted for us. We still had to acquaint ourselves with the protocol for this. How would we contact the bridge keepers and lockkeepers? Would they speak English? We had been told that bridge keepers would lower a Dutch clog on a fishing line for us to put our toll into. How would we know how much to pay?

Whilst we were now quite familiar with the French waterways, and using French locks, Holland was going to be different. Frankly I was nervous because of our limited experience of the country. I thought John was apprehensive too but he was hiding it well and anyway he would have died rather than admit it. He is the kind of person who likes to know exactly what he is doing and examines all aspects of a problem until he is in control both of himself and his surroundings.

Whilst the rain had kept us inside John, an experienced electrical engineer, had been examining the boat's electrics and muttering to himself as he saw the rather amateurish state of it all. He had already begun to replace some of the wiring. Soon it would be to his standard. I had been having a look at the domestic side of things, particularly the galley equipment, and had re-organised the cupboards and lockers. Soon they would be to my standard. We had already amassed several boxes of 'things to take home'.

The rain had begun the day before, following on from two days of cloud and weak sunshine. We had arrived on Monday the previous week after a flight from Liverpool to

Amsterdam, a half hour's train ride to the nearby town of Putten and a taxi ride to Strand Nulde where *Liberty* was waiting for us in her home marina. Nulde was in Gelderland, one of the oldest and largest of the Dutch provinces and as the crow flies we were not far from Amsterdam. We were very comfortable in the marina. There were showers, washing machines and all the facilities we needed – except shops, and fuel. Our first priority had been to get food. During a hasty dash through Schipol airport I had been able to grab a few things at a classy supermarket, which was horribly expensive, but I wasn't counting. The need to have some basic foodstuffs had overridden my need to count the pennies.

In Nulde, where we arrived at 15.00 hrs I went behind the marina to the petrol station which had a small shop attached. They sold bread, milk, butter, etc. as well as basic breakfast cereals, soft drinks and a nice line in sandwiches, so we had not starved for a day or two. However for the first time in my life I tasted buttermilk which I had bought in mistake for fresh milk. It was an acquired taste I thought, but not in tea or coffee. A trip to a larger supermarket would soon be necessary. Normally we would have had bikes with us but we had not been able to bring them on the plane. The airline had allowed bicycles, but only within the basic weight allowance, and we had both felt that excluding our shoes, pyjamas and other comforts wasn't really worth the extra mobility.

We did not know anyone in the marina but had made the acquaintance of the harbourmaster a jolly fair-haired chap in red jersey and a red knitted hat, looking rather like a roving navigation marker. He spoke a little English and we hoped he might offer a lift into town when we enquired whether there were buses. Our enquiry brought a negative response and no offer of the hoped-for lift. Most Dutch people speak a little English and I had enquired of a woman I had met in the shower block. I understood her to say that there was a supermarket ½ km beyond the railway station. The station was roughly four kilometres away, half way between the marina and the nearest town of Putten. It would be a comfortable walk but we enjoy walking. We set off soon after breakfast on Friday and it started to rain just as we left the boat. We had our waterproofs on and were not worried but that turned out to be ill-founded travellers' optimism. By the time we reached the point of no return the sky was releasing a torrential downpour. It ran off our waterproofs and saturated our trousers; it pervaded our shoes and soaked our socks. My waterproof was not equal to such rain and my rugby shirt was soon very damp and cold and my trousers dark with rain. I began to feel wet, chilled and miserable and longed for the sight of the supermarket.

We trudged along just putting one foot in front of the other, beneath trees which scattered huge cold drops onto our heads, but grateful that there were no hills in this part of Holland. How glad we were to see the railway station, and eventually a red and yellow supermarket sign swinging above the premises which seemed to us like a welcoming beacon. Our hearts lifted and we quickened our steps. I felt in my pocket for my shopping list, hoping that it had not turned into soggy pulp. But, imagine our feelings when the 'supermarket' turned out to be devoted to selling gardening equipment and tools with not a scrap of food in sight unless you counted the sweets at the checkout. We were speechless for a few moments. But we counted our blessings, at least it was dry and we gladly embraced its warmth, wandering round buying paint brushes, electrical sockets and wiring, a hole-saw and one or two other necessities, whilst our dripping waterproofs hung over our trolley to dry. We learned from the check-out assistant that the nearest supermarket was in Putten. After we had made our purchases we poked our noses outside and discovered that the rain had stopped and we said 'in for a penny, in for a pound' and set off to walk the further 3-4 kilometres into the town along flat, tree-lined roads, dotted with the occasional neat bungalow. Once there we found not only a supermarket but all the facilities of a small town. Neat little Dutch houses of red brick, with equally neat front gardens lined brick-cobbled streets. The main street was pedestrianised and full of the 'lifestyle' shops so beloved of the Netherlanders, selling candles and wicker baskets, glassware and household ornaments. There were also cafés and newsagents, a post office, and a bank. All within walking distance of each other along the main street. Putten was an old town of 23,000 inhabitants and its name is thought to derive from the Dutch word *Putheim*, meaning 'house near a well'.

It was hard to appreciate that it was an old town as everything was so orderly, clean and new looking. There was no litter, the gardens were well cared for and even the rubbish bins seemed to be standing neatly to attention.

We bought a Dutch SIM card for our mobile phone before heading for a cosy tea-shop where we enjoyed a *Croque Monsieur*. These toasty cheese and ham sandwiches make a delightful lunch. We then tackled the supermarket, loading a groaning trolley with everything we could possibly need for the next week at least. When the trolley could hold no more we paid our bill, and the young woman at Customer Services called a taxi for us. We rode back to the harbour in style and completely dry.

We had had another problem to deal with when we first arrived on *Liberty*. Whilst she had been standing waiting for us to come and take possession of her a family of coots had decided to become squatters on our bathing platform. They had built a very complicated nest which was intertwined with the bathing ladder. It contained a variety of sweet wrappers and bits of plastic, interwoven with the twigs, and sitting in the middle were three eggs. We did not know what to do. We obviously could not stay around to wait until the eggs hatched, nor could we detach the nest without destroying it completely. The kindest thing we could think of was to destroy the nest now whilst the coots still had plenty of time to build another nest and lay more eggs. We apologised profusely to them but of course they had no idea what we were saying, and clucked and squawked furiously at John as he dismembered their nest. As soon as it was done they came back and tried to re-build it. We had to tie some fenders to the bottom of our ladder to discourage them. I was very, very sad and watched them carefully for the next few days whilst they chose another boat and began the process all over again. I am so sorry Mrs. Coot.

On Saturday we had found another excuse to stay. It was "Harbour Day". We were not quite sure what that would be, but hoped for some camaraderie with our fellow boat owners. It was heralded by the arrival of a giant 'Bouncy Castle' unloaded from the back of a lorry by several strong men onto a patch of green grass by the harbour office. This kept the children happy and excited all day. Their cries echoed around the harbour, especially when a thick pole was suspended horizontally over a section of the water and the children took it in turns to belabour each other with inflated fenders with the inevitable very wet result.

The weather was warm but occasional rain showers sent everyone scurrying for shelter, and temporarily silenced the enthusiastic woman with the microphone who was organising the games.

For the adults there was a small Boat Jumble where we could have disposed of some of our unwanted gear had we known about it in advance. As it was we added to our gear by buying a small clock to fasten to the bulkhead over our bed.

Many of the boats were 'dressed overall' and made a fine sight with red white and blue bunting fluttering from stem to stern.

The main attraction for the adults appeared to be eel-smoking. An oven was set up on the quayside from which this Dutch treat, known as *gerokt paling*, was produced, and the eels were consumed at nearby tables in large quantities. Whilst the Dutch people seem to find them irresistible we could not face them ourselves.

In the evening there was music and a disco which interestingly played mostly English pop songs, but played them very loudly. We went along in the hope of making some new friends but Klaas and Kitty, from whom we had bought *Liberty*, could only come for part of the afternoon and without them to act as translators in the evening we were very much on our own.

We were quite surprised that no one joined us at our table as we had found the Dutch to be very friendly. On the day we had first decided to buy *Liberty*, Klaas and Kitty had invited us to join them that evening in the marina bar where there was a practice for the male voice choir of which Klaas was a member, and which specialised in singing sea-shanties. When the choir members discovered that we were British they included some English songs in their repertoire, and in the interval and at the end, many of the choir members were eager to practise their English and tell us their experiences of visiting our country. They insisted on buying us drinks and we felt very welcomed and included. We learned that this type of male voice choir was as popular in Holland as it was in Wales, and Klaas and Kitty gave us a CD of their songs.

On this occasion everyone seemed to be in groups of friends and intent on consuming as much alcohol, mainly beer, as they could. There was much laughter and revelry but no drunkenness. We saw no one we recognised from the choir practice. We even attempted a turn on the dance floor but the volume of the music sent us scurrying to an outside table, and after sitting alone nursing gin and tonics, being gradually deafened, we finally retreated from the noise.

Groups of revellers sat late into the night at picnic tables arranged around the marina, they chatted and laughed but were not too noisy.

The weather continued changeable all week. We had occasional meals on our rear deck but mostly we were indoors.

The boat was very comfortable, and well appointed. It was full of knick-knacks such as china windmills and clogs, wooden ducks, a model boat and an 8" high figure of a fisherman (which we had named Cap'n Bob), not to mention assorted brassware and artificial plants. There were also three brass lamps – one electric and the others oil, all very beautiful but a little over the top. Gradually I would decide which of these I wanted to keep and pass the rest on to someone who would appreciate them more than I.

We were pleased with *Liberty*. We found her very spacious and when we were confined indoors because of rain there was room for us to move about and get on with things, whereas in our sailing boat we were always treading on each other's feet. I particularly loved the little diesel stove with a chimney that went up through the roof. When this was lit we were wonderfully cosy.

To help us plan our route and increase our confidence we needed some more charts and sailing instructions. Jan, the harbourmaster, told us that there would be a chandlery at our first stop, Harderwijk.

To reach Harderwijk we had to motor down a long thin lake; the Randmeren which, I think, translates as rim lake. This follows the contours of Gelderland and divides it from Flevoland, the newest Dutch province which was created entirely out of water, sandbanks and mud flats, as a result of massive land reclamation in 1967. The Dutch have been battling with the sea for 1000 years and were justifiably proud of their achievements. No wonder so many of the towns seem new, they were. Every house, hedge, canal, field, garden and road in this province was 4 metres below sea level. A booklet had been published by the Netherlands Ministry of Transport and Public Works. In it was the quotation "The French once said that God made the world, but the Dutch made their own country. Although this is somewhat of an exaggeration, we consider that the French were right."

Experiment had shown that a continuous band of deep water around a polder maintained the correct ground-water table in the neighbouring 'old' land. This was good news for the thousands of boat owners in the Netherlands. There were now 4,400 kilometres of navigable waterway in the country and there is no country in the world in which it is so easy to travel by boat from the centre of a town into the countryside. The Randmeren had been developed as recreational area of water with carefully landscaped banks and many facilities – for fishing, bathing, cruising, caravanning and camping.

The amenities for boat owners are continually being extended and there appeared to be no shortage of harbours where we would find mooring space along our route. Sailing seems to be well regulated in Holland and our reading matter gave us a list of requirements which included the need to have a VHF radio on board and to keep a listening watch at all times. This worried us a little as, although we had a hand-held VHF with us we had left the certificates which allowed us to use this at home and had not yet obtained a radio licence for *Liberty*. We had hoped to keep the radio in a locker and only use it for emergencies. But in other respects we believed we complied with the regulations, after all *Liberty* has been sailed in Dutch waters for the last thirty years so she must meet the specifications. Come to think of it then, where was the VHF radio?

We had decided that we must set off soon. We had filled the store cupboard, familiarised ourselves with the workings of the boat and worked out our route to France. We were going to go north on the Randmeren to Ketelmere on the edge of the IJsselmere. Then we would turn south down the IJssel river and follow it to Arnhem. At Arnhem we would take the Pannerdens canal on the Rhine and connect up with the Waal. From there another canal would lead into the Maas, which would take us into Belgium, and on to where it becomes the Meuse, thus taking us into France. Whilst all the charts were in Dutch one had an English translation of the symbols and we had made copious notes. We had also studied the local chart and had familiarised ourselves with the route to Harderwijk. It seemed quite straightforward. We paid our harbour dues and had no more reasons to stay.

We finally decided to leave on Wednesday. Klaas and Kitty had visited the day before to say farewell and brought with them a beautiful plant, a tall orange daisy in a square terracotta pot. It now graced the wheelhouse. In return I gave them a tea-towel from Lancashire which co-incidentally had a canal boat (Leeds-Liverpool canal) and a windmill (Lytham-St-Anne's) on it.

When morning dawned it was raining, and it continued to rain. I was very disappointed, having made the decision to leave it now seemed as though we would be thwarted. We had an inside as well as an outside steering position but we had not planned to use the inside one until we were confident in handling *Liberty*. Visibility was far better outside. There seemed little point in setting out in the rain when we could not see our surroundings properly and would be getting soaked into the bargain. But we felt that if we did not get away soon we would be putting down roots.

But by 10.30 the rain had stopped and a weak sun began to emerge. Hurrah, we could go. Casting off was rather scary. Would we be able to handle this new monohull? Would we find our way to the next harbour? Would we be able to understand the Dutch charts? Would there be room in the next harbour, and after Harderwijk, what then? The moorings were strange too. Would they all be like this? Instead of mooring the boat alongside a quay, or even going bows-to as we had been used to doing with *Chefren* in the Mediterranean, the moorings here were thick trunks of trees, or piles, upright in the water, two or three along each side of the boat. You steer the boat between them like putting a cow into a stall, and throw a prepared rope over the corner posts. Our learning curve was shooting up steeply.

It all seemed so strange and new - new boat, new type of boat, new moorings and new country. But if you want to eat something as big as an elephant there is only one way to do it – a bite at a time. So we did all the things we were accustomed to doing on our catamaran – removed the electric cable from the shore socket, prepared the lines for casting off and readied the fenders. John started the engine, I slipped the lines, fended us off the pile moorings and we reversed effortlessly out of our space, so far so good.

My stomach was churning and my knees felt weak as we turned across the marina to the entrance and headed out into the Randmeren. I did not know whether this was nervousness or excitement. Perhaps it was a little of both. John was not saying much and was trying to look confident, standing at the helm with his navy-blue sailor's cap at a jaunty angle.

We saw another motorboat leaving its moorings at the same time and slowed down to let them get ahead. It would make life so much easier if we could follow another boat. But we found the channel clearly marked, each buoy numbered and in the place it should be. We began to relax. John steered the boat and I counted off the numbers on the buoys, checking our location and looking out for the various things mentioned on the chart.

The journey took a couple of hours. The landscape

was largely flat and featureless but it was interesting to see the other boats. There were small yachts, traditional Dutch sailing boats (*botters*), modern motorboats, trip boats, huge sea going craft and a rusting dredger. We passed close to the botter and admired the red canvas sails, and I asked John about the huge lee-boards attached at each side like the wings of a pre-historic monster. He explained that these can be lowered into the water to prevent the boat being pushed sideways by the wind (to lee-ward, in fact). We passed a *reddingsbridgade* (life-boat station), and there was also a string of small sailing dinghies pulled by a lead boat with an outboard motor. In them were Dutch sea scouts out for a day on the Randmeren which by now had widened into a large lake. We looked about us with interest.

Soon the blue dome of the Dolphinarium at Harderwijk came into view and I counted off the buoys to find the channel which would take us into the harbour. We aimed to moor as close to the town as possible so that we could shop and stock up with more food and chandlery, and do some sight-seeing. We were also hoping to have a day in Amsterdam from here. It would have been a pity to be in Holland and not visit the cultural capital, especially as John had not been there before.

The motorboat we had followed from Nulde came to our aid again, tying alongside the town quay where there was space for us also, and we made our lines fast to the mooring rings. When we were settled and eating our lunch on the rear deck Jan, the harbourmaster from Nulde, together with his wife, came past in their boat and tied up further down the quay. Later, when we were on our way to the shops we passed their boat and exchanged waves. They were moored close to a lifting bridge giving access to a small harbour where several old Dutch fishing and sailing boats and some interesting house boats were moored. It was just like the pictures in my child-hood story books. Alongside was a windmill sporting a sign saying 'Mill Open' which was just as well because at that moment the heavens opened and we raced across the little square and took refuge inside the mill. It proved an interesting visit. This three-stage mill had been reconstructed from parts of other mills around the country and added a picturesque touch to the harbour front. It had working sails and a thatched roof. The view over the surrounding countryside was spectacular if a little damp. Our visit was instructive and informative and kept us dry until the rain eased off. A young family were also visiting the mill and the three year old in the party was keen on increasing her vocabulary. She had just learned the Dutch word for mill and at every stage she was repeating "*Molen, molen*" with great delight. As we too wanted to increase our range of Dutch words we added it to our mental vocabulary and from this point whenever we saw a windmill we shouted "Molen, molen!"

We continued shopping when the rain had eased. Our first priority was to find the necessary charts. There was a branch of the ANWB in Harderwijk as there is in most Dutch towns. This is the Dutch equivalent of the AA but as there

were as many waterways as roads in the Netherlands, and as 85% of the population have bicycles they also sell charts and information about sailing, and about cycle routes and ferries etc. We found their well-stocked shop and with the help of an English-speaking customer we soon had what we needed.

The Netherlands are almost completely flat and cycling is very popular. Whenever they have time and the weather is suitable the Dutch people head outdoors. All the towns have cycle paths, and many have separate sets of traffic lights for the cyclists. Boating is also popular. The English have caravans, the Dutch have boats. A number of them are huge expensive affairs and we saw many of them later in France, and learned that the Dutch are not allowed to buy second homes, perhaps this was because of the shortage of land. Instead they buy boats.

It was not difficult to get the other things we needed in the shops but paying for them was. Our English credit card was rejected at all the shops except the ANWB. We had to pay by cash and then had a long walk to find a cash machine and draw out enough money to last us for several days. We discovered that the Rabobank was the only one whose cash machines would accept our card. We found this was the norm throughout the Netherlands, only international shops were able to accept our English credit card.

Many Dutch words were very similar to English, so we found communication quite easy. I had bought a Dutch/English dictionary to help the process and discovered that shops were called *winkels*, and a sweet shop was a *snoep winkel*. What a lovely language. It sounded like something out of a children's book. To my mind a snoep winkel would be a tiny shop with bottle glass in its windows with an aged shop keeper with white hair and steel rimmed glasses presiding over jars of brightly coloured boiled sweets. Instead I found a very modern, supermarket style of shop with trays of pick 'n' mix filled with fluorescent liquorice, huge jelly babies, paper wrapped humbugs, and yes, some boiled sweets. Modern boxes of chocolate and candy lined the shelves and brightly coloured party balloons festooned the doorway and the ceiling.

Walking back from the shops we found that several boats had left and we had a clear view of *Liberty* at the end of the harbour, moored by the statue of a mermaid who was perched on the quay with her fishtail hanging over the edge. We were able to see the flared bow of the boat and her clean lines. She looked very fine and I had a lump in my throat when I realised that I was part-owner of that smart boat.

But the disappearance of the other boats had revealed a notice which informed us that this quay was reserved for the *Prins Willem Alexander*. Did this mean we would have to move? We wanted to leave *Liberty* the next day and go into Amsterdam, so it might be a problem. I walked down the quay looking for another space and came to the boat belonging to Jan. I decided to ask his advice and knocked on the hull. He informed me that the *Prins Willem Alexander*, whilst being a huge hotel boat, did not come very often In any case the Harderwijk harbourmaster would soon be round for some money and I would be able to ask. Sure enough a young woman came later to collect our payment and assured us that the *Willem Alexander* would not be coming that night or the next.

CHAPTER 2 – Changing Boats

Anticipation

Originally we had not intended to give up our sailing in the Mediterranean quite so soon, although we had known for some time that it was 'on the cards'. Then a series of circumstances brought us to the south coast of France and we decided to take *Chefren* back home through the canals and made the decision that if we enjoyed this trip as much as the first one, we would sell *Chefren* and get a canal boat.

We entered the system at Port St. Louis du Rhône at the bottom of the river Rhône, where we had her mast removed and laid along the deck. It would not be possible to pass under the bridges further north with our mast up, and there are few lifting bridges in France. We sailed *Chefren* as far as St. Jean de Losne in the centre of France where we left her until the following spring. France was just as delightful as we had remembered and the decision was made to take *Chefren* home and put her into brokerage.

Before returning for *Chefren* the following year we had begun our search for her replacement. We had been told that the best and cheapest motor cruisers were to be found in Holland chiefly because there are so many boats there. We researched suitable Internet sites, and drew up a list of things that we would want on a new boat. On each site we visited we looked for pictures of the right sort of vessels in our price range and printed off the details.

Many of the specification lists were in Dutch but most of the words were easy to understand such as *anker, boot, diepte* and *kiel* (anchor, boat, depth and keel). Soon our dining-room table was awash with files of specifications and pictures from which we discarded those which did not meet our requirements. John was reluctantly making the change from a sailing boat to a motorboat and one of his specifications was that it should have an anchor and instrumentation; that would make it capable of going to sea should we decide we wanted to visit any of the French offshore islands, such as the Porquerolles, or even Corsica. My main requirements were a roomy galley, a separate cabin for us with hanging lockers, and a shower.

We went to a local bookshop and bought a road map of the Netherlands and began to circle the places where boats on our short list were to be found and to plan an itinerary.

As Easter approached we had a list of eighteen boats and planned to spend the Easter week-end looking at those within driving distance of Amsterdam. After booking our flight we emailed the boat brokers or boat owners and arranged our visits. There were already a couple of possibilities which I liked the look of, *Liberty* being one of them, and I began to get excited. I reckoned that, allowing for travelling, we could view four or five boats per day. We flew to Amsterdam by an evening flight and had pre-booked a hotel at Aalmere from where we planned to begin our viewing. Everything seemed straightforward but we had not reckoned on a combination of factors. I could not read the map in the darkness of the car interior, it rained continually so we could scarcely read the sign boards outside the car; and the unusual Dutch terrain meant that if we took a wrong turn we could not take a short cut to where we wanted to be, there was usually a dyke in the way and we had to find a bridge. We pulled up in a town square desperately searching for a clue as to where we were. As we did so we heard cheerful voices coming from a lighted doorway. I ventured inside and discovered a sailing club and one of the members very kindly led us in her car to the door of our hotel. We had actually passed the end of the road leading to it three times.

When we began our boat viewing the next day we each found a boat which we liked, but not the same one. John's choice was a boat with a well maintained engine; mine had an interesting internal layout. We carried on south towards Rotterdam, viewing boats as we went and then turning north to Hardersluis. Occasionally a broker would offer us a viewing of a boat that had not been on our list and we would include this before heading off to the next place. On the second day we went from Hardersluis to Strand Nulde where we viewed *Liberty*. She was in private ownership and the owners, Klaas and Kitty, were aboard with coffee brewing for us. After stepping inside I began to feel that our search might be over. My heart quickened. She was just what we were looking for and at just the price we wanted to pay. She was in immaculate condition with light oak varnished woodwork, new red upholstery and cream curtains, with a second toilet in the owners' cabin at the rear. The galley and heads were tiled in grey ceramic tiles with a stainless steel sink in the galley. The engine was reasonably accessible under the floor of the wheelhouse and seemed well maintained. Externally she sported a coat of brilliant white paint with grey decks and an image of the Statue of Liberty on her bows. We fell so in love with her we were prepared to overlook the fact that she had no oven in the galley, just a hob, and there was no shower. We felt these were problems we could overcome later.

Klaas and Kitty did not speak much English and it was difficult to ask them questions about the boat's history, or how things worked. This proved a bit of a problem. But they were lovely people and the harbourmaster's wife was brought in to act as interpreter.

Klaas was a stocky man with twinkling eyes behind rimless glasses who would have looked quite at home in traditional Dutch dress. Kitty was slim and blonde. When she was not brewing cups of aromatic coffee she could be found in the wheelhouse having a quick cigarette. We found that huge numbers of Dutch people still smoke, particularly the women. Klaas had given up after a severe heart attack which required by-pass surgery and that was why they were selling their boat

Liberty was the tenth boat we had viewed and we decided not to look any further. We made arrangements with the harbourmaster for him to haul *Liberty* out of the water for a survey, and arranged for us to receive a contract and documentation by e-mail. There was a hotel within walking distance of the harbour and we booked in for that night, returning later to listen to the choir practice as I mentioned in the first chapter.

The next part of the deal was done over the Internet. Klaas sent a copy of a contract, but of course it was in Dutch. I tried contacting one or two translation companies but the price quoted seemed prohibitive. I wondered if there were any Dutch-speaking people locally and enquired at the library if there might be a "Dutch Circle", or some similar organisation of Dutch speaking people. The librarian told me about a website called Babelfish where I was able to translate the contract myself and make a copy in English. Some of the language seemed a little fractured but we were able to make sense of it. I typed out a copy in English for Klaas.

The survey did not turn up any major problems and Klaas undertook to rectify those that were indicated, including modernising some of the gas installation and obtaining a certificate from a Dutch gas expert. By now we were so excited that we did overlook one or two things which later proved larger problems, involving work and effort on our part. One was the outlet from the sink, which was under the water line, and the surveyor pointed out that this was of plastic and should be changed. When we visited *Liberty* again we discovered that not only was it made of plastic it did not have a shut-off valve so it could be dangerous and might let in water. The other problem was that some of the anti-slip coating on the decks was lifting. We assumed wrongly that this was an adhesive strip which would need gluing. But it was anti-slip paint and the following year we had to remove the entire coat of paint from the deck and re-do it, a long and arduous job.

But these problems were in the future. For now we still had to pay for *Liberty* and the best way seemed to be with a cheque in Euros which the bank arranged for us. Rather than send this in the post we decided to hand it over in person, whilst at the same time signing the contract. We had already booked flights to France in a few weeks time so that we could collect *Chefren* and bring her back to England. We changed those flights and flew instead to Amsterdam, planning to go on to France by train.

Klaas and Kitty met us at the airport and took us to *Liberty* where we were joined by Kitty's sister-in-law. She acted as interpreter as we all sat around the little table in the dinette with more cups of coffee, and we signed and witnessed the contract. We slept aboard *Liberty* for a couple of nights. Kitty had stocked the fridge for us, what a treat. She had left Dutch bacon of the kind that you do not see in England these days. It fried to a crisp with no water in the pan. We had bacon and eggs for tea. There was also a fresh loaf of Dutch bread, and some golden butter.

The next day Klaas came for us and took us to their home in Soest for a champagne lunch. We felt we had made some good friends. I had taken them a hamper of English goodies such as home-made chutneys, jams, fudge, all tied up with a big ribbon. Klaas cooked delicious pork fillet in pepper sauce, served with a crisp green salad and more crusty Dutch bread. Afterwards we sat in their neat garden attempting to talk to each other across the language barrier. They had an English speaking neighbour who came in when he had finished work and oiled the wheels of communication.

We discovered that Klaas and Kitty were also second-time-arounders, having been married only five years. Kitty was still working at the food processing factory where they met, but Klaas had retired.

They told us that the town in which they live, Soest, was the home of Queen Beatrix, queen of the Netherlands, who can often be seen riding around on her bicycle. Imagine seeing the Queen of England cycling around London instead of riding in a limousine. If she did it would make her more human and accessible. The Dutch seem to regard their monarchy with the affection reserved for favourite family members.

Our next task was to deliver *Chefren* to England and put her up for sale, then come back to Holland for *Liberty*. In the meantime *Liberty* would remain on her present mooring.

The following day Klaas kindly ran us to the station at Amersfoort, from where we caught a train to Amsterdam and on into France.

We needed to change trains at Lille onto the TGV (*Train de Grande Vitesse*), the high speed train which would deliver us to Dijon at 21.00 where we planned to spend another night before taking the slow shuttle train to where we had left *Chefren*. It was a great plan which I had conceived, again with the help of the Internet, and should have been an easy journey. But we had reckoned without an accident on the line which required us to disembark at Lorken in Flanders, from where we were directed to another platform and another train. The instructions were in Flemish and we had to ask another passenger to translate. What no one told us was that we needed to change again in order to reach Lille. We knew we would not make our connection in time now and the journey seemed interminable. The train we were on was going to Boulogne and I said to John, "My geography is not wonderful but I do not think Boulogne is near Lille." It is not. When we disembarked we were fortunate to find an English-speaking porter who told us that we would be able to get a train to Lille in half an hour. Just time to grab a sandwich from the station buffet, and we were on our way again. We discovered later that we had probably travelled 90 kilometres further than needed.

In Lille we arrived at a very modern glass and steel station complex, part of a bold and ostentatious business district housing two railway stations, a shopping centre and cafés, known as Eurolille. We presented ourselves at the booking office and explained our plight. The very helpful young man told us that there were no more trains to Dijon that night and we could either take the slow train and change in Paris the next morning, or wait until evening and get the same time TGV as we should have caught today. He offered to book us into a hotel. We accepted his offer of the hotel booking and opted for the TGV. By now we were very tired and it was raining again. We trundled our luggage through the streets of Lille and found our hotel about 15 mins from the station.

The next day we had the bonus of an unexpected day in Lille but because it continued to rain we wanted to be under cover. A visit to the tourist office, housed in a Burgundian palace, provided us with a map and details of the Palais de Beaux Arts, a museum second only to the Louvre in Paris. We spent the morning in the ceramics section gazing at ancient statuary and a wonderful array of old porcelain. It was possible to gain a feel for the social history of the various centuries by studying the table ware, porcelain plaques and pictures, snuff boxes and so on. Even John, the non-sightseer, became absorbed.

By lunchtime the rain had eased and we decided to have a wander through Lille and in particular to walk to the river front and see whether it was somewhere we might want to come by boat.

Lille is the capital of French Flanders and is a European crossroads boasting the Eurostar terminal, built in 1994, which now goes as far as Paris, and a TGV link opened in 1993. It is the fourth largest city in France and close to the Belgian border. I had to keep reminding myself that I was now in France, not in Flanders. The city had a strong Flemish feel from its architecture to its cuisine. It was once part of the Spanish Netherlands but has been French since 1667. In 2004 it was nominated the European capital of culture something of which the citizens are rightly proud.

The section of the river which we eventually found looked rather depressing after the rain and we got the impression that it was not much used by pleasure craft although Lille does have a busy harbour area. Perhaps we had come to the wrong part. We found a disused lock and moorings for trip boats close to a grassy area but the port de plaisance must have been in a different part of the city.

Making our way back to the station complex we were eventually whisked by the TGV to Dijon, the mustard capital of France, but because we had already had one night's delay we decided to take a taxi immediately to the marina where we had left *Chefren*. I always leave the bedding in dry-bags and there would be no problem making up our beds and sleeping aboard, even though it would be late evening, or would there?

We trundled our luggage along the marina pontoon and our hearts lifted at the sight of *Chefren* at her mooring. We have had many happy times aboard her and we have become very attached. It was going to be a wrench to sell her.

As we drew near we thought she seemed a little lower

in the water than when we had left her, and this was confirmed when I stepped ahead of John into the cockpit and found it full of water. Gingerly I unlocked the door and reached inside the boat for the torch we had left there. Shining it into the cabin I was met with a reflection of the beam. John joined me and we peered into the interior where our berth cushions were standing on end in a foot of black, smelly water, a plastic sandal floated by the table leg. The whole of the central cabin of the boat was awash. The hulls to either side had so far escaped and I was able to step across to one hull, descend the three steps to floor level there and reach our wellies from a locker in the stern cabin. John went into the other hull and found a couple of buckets and we began baling out. What a thing to greet us. From the state of the cockpit it became clear that leaves, sycamore seeds, and general detritus as well as melting snow had blocked the cockpit drains over the winter. Obviously no one had checked her or noticed that she was beginning to sink. The water had gradually seeped into the boat and filled the central bilge which had then overflowed to fill the main cabin.

I decided to go in search of one of the marina staff and confront them with the evidence of what I saw as their neglect. There was no harbourmaster at this marina but someone from another boat had a phone number of one of the owners who arrived quickly bringing a huge pump. By that time John had found our own little electric pump and set it working and the boat was almost empty. When the marina owner saw the mess he said,

"You won't be able to sleep in there tonight; you had better go to the hotel".

"Who will pay for that?" I asked, "Will the marina pay?"

"Why should we do that?" he retorted.

"Because we have been paying you to look after our boat."

Without another word he picked up his pump and left the boat.

John and I looked at each other in stunned silence. We locked up *Chefren*, picked up our bags, and with heavy hearts set off in search of a hotel. The little town of St Jean de Losne is actually two towns, St. Jean and Losne which straddle the river Saône. There are bridges over the canal which joins the Saône here as well as the bridge over the river, and whilst we had been told that there was a hotel 'over the bridge' we did not know which bridge. We crossed the first bridge we came to, which was the canal bridge and found ourselves wandering along a narrow street where one or two houses still had lights on. At one house a woman was washing-up at an open window overlooking the street. "Excuse me," I ventured in my best schoolgirl French, "Where is the hotel?"

She came out to talk to us and explained that the hotel was across the river bridge, a kilometre away, and would probably be closed by now. "But I know the proprietor," she said. "I will phone and ask him to open up for you".

A moment or two later she returned with the good news that the hotel was being opened up, it was by now nearing midnight, and that if we would wait another moment she would get her car out and drive us there. We were staggered at such kindness and pressed effusive thanks upon her as we disembarked at a small *auberge* on the Losne side of the river.

The proprietor signed us in and showed us to a pleasant room with en suite facilities overlooking the river. We asked him about the possibility of getting something to eat as we had not eaten since lunch. Despite the lateness of the hour he provided us with a cold repast that was fit to feed the gods. There was a baguette of crusty French bread, pats of yellow butter, a savoury pâté en croute, firm golden cheese, mouth watering apple tart and a bottle of wine, all of which he served on a tray in our room.

The following day we set about getting all the wet carpet and upholstery out of *Chefren* and surveying the extent of the damage. Water had penetrated our heater and our CD/radio, neither of which would ever work again. The foam cushions were covered in mould, the carpet dripped with filthy water, the walls and curtains were spotted with mildew - as was our wet weather gear, and my straw hat which had been hanging in one of the small cabins was an unrecognisable green furred mass

Fortunately we had brought with us from home a small steam cleaner. As we were going to put *Chefren* up for sale I had wanted to give her a good clean out before we left her in England. How fortuitous. It cleaned up the carpets and the walls beautifully but the whole process took several days.

We had arrived on a bank holiday weekend and I knew no one would be at work at our insurers but I contacted the emergency number. I was able to speak to a young woman who took all the details and eventually rang back to say that a surveyor would be with us on the afternoon of the first working day, Tuesday. It was a coincidence that an English surveyor was coming over to France that day to do another job at a marina just an hour away.

We take our hats off to our insurers. The surveyor was able to give us immediate instructions to order new cushions and anything else we might need to make the boat habitable again. He listed and photographed everything. I had also photographed things on the first day and was able to show him these photos. All the facilities needed to put *Chefren* back together again were available in the little town and we were ready to go after a week. The final claim was settled without problems soon after we returned home.

Whilst we cleaned *Chefren* up we stayed in a hotel. Unfortunately the auberge did not have a room available for subsequent nights but the tourist office provided us with the address of a local pub which had rooms available, and whilst this was not quite as luxurious it was character filled. The pub itself fronted the river Saône, and its rooms were in another building behind the bar, an old building which had recently been converted. We were the only guests at that time and had our own key to come and go as we wanted. I found it strange that the auberge should be full, but this establishment was empty. It was an eerie feeling letting ourselves into an empty building each night. But it was clean and comfortable enough and cheaper than the auberge. We had ensuite facilities but they were only separated from our sleeping area by a curtain. Our bed was covered with a chintz bedspread matching the curtains which framed our view of the river. We ate our meals on *Chefren* as the galley was untouched but we usually began the day with coffee and a croissant at a beer-stained bar table, where a grinning boar's head surveyed us from alongside the beer pumps. I am not sure what the proprietor and his wife made of the English couple who disappeared every day in working clothes. We were very grateful for our shower when we returned each evening, washing off the grime and sweat from our exertions on *Chefren*.

When we finally set off to deliver *Chefren* to England, we got underway each day as soon as the locks were open at 08.30 and travelled until the locks closed at 18.30, eating lunch on the move. We reached the coast at St. Valéry in two weeks which was quite good time. We had been through 266 locks and travelled for 643 kilometres. Had we not been in a hurry we would have expected to take six weeks over this journey. Most of he locks were only five metres wide and *Chefren* was 4.7 metres wide, it was a tight fit  but John was very skilled at steering us in, with my hand signals from the bow.

The journey was hard and often cold as we now had no heater. One morning we woke to find snow on the deck and very often there was frost on the insides of the windows. It was a very cold journey which became an endurance test.

We were delayed on only one occasion when we found ourselves behind a slow-moving, laden peniche. At the end of the day we were moored behind it, together with a French boat, just outside the lock at St. Dizier. The skipper from the French boat went up to the lock and asked the lockkeeper to enquire of the skipper of the peniche whether both our boats might go through first in the morning as we were travelling at a faster rate. She told him that the peniche skipper was insisting on his rights to go first. We ground our teeth in frustration, but had our revenge when the peniche went aground as he exited the lock. The lockkeeper had to fill and empty the lock once or twice to get enough water through to re-float the peniche. If he had allowed us to go first there might already have been enough water for him. It served him right. Whilst we waited for the peniche to get well ahead of us the couple on the French boat invited us for lunch. They were Daniel and Alain who live just outside Paris and had been to collect a new Nicholls cruiser from the Nicholls' base on the Saône. I was very envious of their boat, particularly because they had heating, and because they had an inside steering position. Daniel drove it like a car. Alain was the cook and the meal he prepared was endive wrapped in bacon and served with a cheese sauce. We had never eaten endive before and found it delicious. The Nicholls was a beautiful boat with well appointed insides. They had a full size cooker (with oven) and a huge fridge/freezer. Their sleeping cabins were below decks and I know they had at least one shower down there. But outside there were very narrow side decks with tiny guard rails, it was designed rather like a car. Getting on and off was not easy as one had to use a step set into the bodywork by the back deck, and the narrrow side decks meant that it was not easy to get ropes onto the bollards. Daniel tended to pull up alongside the lock ladder from where Alain would climb to the lockside to tie on his ropes. I thought we were going to find *Liberty* a lot easier to use.

We travelled with Daniel and Alain as far as Chalons en Champagne and whenever we had to wait for a slow lock Alain would take pity on us and invite us into their warm boat for a coffee.

We had another slightly hazardous incident when we came to a lifting bridge, with traffic lights. The bridge was lifted for us and traffic was stationery by the bridge, but the lights were at red. We waited to see if the bridge would be lowered but nothing happened. After a long wait we decided that the only thing was to go through the bridge with care, being prepared to stop quickly if the bridge began to descend. I turned to Alain and Daniel in the boat behind and gave what I hoped was a Gallic shrug and we went through without mishap. They followed us through. I do not know how long the traffic was held up before someone came to fix it.

We delivered *Chefren* to Newhaven on the English coast where we left her in brokerage. I nearly cried as we walked away from her, she was so full of memories; the three months we had spent as part of the boating community in Cornwall whilst John re-fitted the galley, and the summers we had spent in Greece floating from island to island in the Ionian, not to mention the journeys up and down the Italian coast on our way to and from Greece. But I was in no doubt we would develop the same kind of relationship with our new boat, *Liberty*, and knew we had that to look forward to.

Chapter 3. Harderwijk to Kampen

Excitement

John, like most men, when he gets behind the wheel of a car or a boat just wants to get to where he is going. Sometimes when we were travelling on a canal I even have had difficulty in getting him to stop for lunch. To me this attitude does not make sense when we are on holiday. I want to stop and 'smell the flowers' and explore the countryside along the way. So we had a little chat and I managed to persuade him to think in terms of being on holiday rather than journeying, and being prepared to stay at each place and discover more about it. We did have an itinerary and a destination on this trip but had many weeks in which to reach it. John had also said that sight-seeing was 'not his bag' but I had found that once I could persuade him to join me in an expedition to somewhere I thought would appeal to him he has taken a keen interest. So now we were planning to visit Amsterdam before we travelled any further. I felt we couldn't visit Holland without seeing its cultural capital. We had thought of making the trip by train from Nulde but the distance of the station from the harbour had put us off. We had expected the station at Harderwijk to be closer. Not so. We were advised to take a bus but being unsure of the times we decided to set off along the bus route, hoping to catch one on our way. I think the distance was even further than to the station at Putten. We walked through the town and into the outskirts and had been walking for ¾ hr. before we found it. We almost gave up. At least the weather was fine; this was proving to be one of the best days we had had so far. It gave us an opportunity to see something of the more modern outskirts of the town and we passed several very modern factories and office blocks, all concrete and glass, surrounded by trees and flowers.

We changed trains at Amersfoort and arrived in Amsterdam just in time for lunch which we ate at a café on Damrak whilst watching the diverse nationalities and characters going past.

I hoped John would be able to gain a brief but accurate impression of the city in one day. We were rather taken with the idea of borrowing one of the two-seater pedal bikes which were whizzing by. They can be borrowed from various points in the city for getting about. But I had a rather more leisurely form of transport in mind, a trip by canal.

The first canals in Amsterdam were built in the 17th century, forming a triple ring, the *Grachtengordel*, for the purpose of moving goods around the city. At that time Amsterdam was a wealthy trading city. This first ring has been extended over the years and now the city is famed for its canals and its elegant waterside mansions and warehouses, many of which have been converted into apartments and cafés.

Early planning laws, unstable topsoil, and plot dimensions constrained the houses to a largely uniform shape and size. They were built of lightweight brick or sandstone with large windows to reduce weight. Owners had therefore stamped their individuality on their homes by the use of decorative gables, cornices, ornate doorframes and varying window shapes. We saw neck gables, step gables, and spout gables to mention but a few. Some still had the carved and painted wall plaques which were used to identify the houses before house numbers were introduced. Many of these depicted the owner's occupation such as a milkmaid with a yoke identifying a dairy producer. Others were decorated with scrolls, coats of arms and crests.

It had also become the custom to build the houses with a slight tilt outwards and to place furniture hooks outside the uppermost window. This was because the houses are so tall and narrow that furniture cannot be carried up the stairs. Instead these hooks were used to lift the furniture in through the windows and the lean was to protect the furniture from damage by contact with the house wall.

Many people in Amsterdam live on houseboats and we passed down *Bowuwersgracht* (Brewers' canal) where many of them are to be found. We also passed along *Herengracht*, once known as the Golden Bend because of the wealthy people who lived there, and on *Singel* we saw the *Poezenboot* which is a houseboat refuge for stray cats.

We travelled through a sea lock and out into the IJssel before eventually turning back into the city where we saw the striking Italian-designed building known as the Nemo, an educational centre for science and technology. It is a huge concrete and glass structure which has been built in the form of a ship overhanging the water by 30 metres (99 feet). I wonder if the architect was conscious of the old tradition of leaning buildings?

One of the memories which remained with us was the sight of a multi-storey bicycle park outside one of the office blocks. There were several levels containing nothing but bicycles, an amazing sight.

Afterwards we walked through the streets and found an English bookshop where we bought a guidebook and a phrase book as well as some English reading matter. At an Internet café we caught up on our e-mails and also the latest news. We were horrified to learn that there had been a terrorist attack on London. The brief news report mentioned an underground train and a double-decker bus. We could not get more news for a few days as the English papers would be a day late in Holland but it sounded dreadful and cast a shadow over our day. I said a prayer for the victims and their families. As we meandered back to the train we saw photographs and headlines in the Dutch papers on the stands.

I think that by now we were getting blasé about travelling around Holland by train, or maybe we were still stunned by the news of the attack on London because we changed trains at Amersfoort without checking and crossed the platform for the Zwolle train which was just leaving. The train on this route goes through Harderwijk, but we found that this particular train did not stop. The ticket collector informed us that we were on the express or *Sneltrain*. Fortunately when we reached Zwolle (about 10 km. further on) there was a stopping train in the other direction and we were soon back where we wanted to be. We discovered and made use of the train taxi from the station. The purpose of this is that the taxi will take several people to different destinations, dropping them off where they want to go, each paying a fixed rate. We were the only people going to the harbour and the lady taxi driver had to phone for permission to take us. We asked to be dropped off by the mermaid on the quay and she confessed that she had lived in Harderwijk all her life and did not know that the mermaid statue was there.

When evening came we telephoned John's children who both work in London. They and their families were all safe for which we were thankful, but our hearts went out to the injured and the families who had lost loved ones in the carnage. We felt very helpless and also guilty that we were not at home at that time.

Spending these few days in Harderwijk had given us the illusion that we had begun our travels, even though we were such a short distance from Nulde. We had taken the first bite of the elephant.

We found it to be a pleasant town, founded in the 12th century, and by the 13th century had become so important because of its trade in dyes and fishing that the local count granted it a charter and ordered fortifications to be built. By the mid seventeenth century the Netherlands was one of the greatest trading nations in the world, a position it gradually relinquished in the eighteenth century. It was an East Indiaman terminal and was regularly visited by the old sailing ship *Amsterdam* which we had seen on our visit to the city. But the harbour went into decline in the 18th century due to the silting up of the Zuiderzee. Harderwijk was once on the edge of the Zuiderzee but was now many kilometres inland. Nowadays one of its main attractions was the Dolphinarium, the largest sea-zoo in Europe.

Remnants of its ancient walls could still be seen, but the town was so beautifully preserved it was difficult to detect which part was old and which was new.

To reach the shops we cut through narrow, brick paved streets, lined with terraced, two-storey houses. The houses fronted straight onto the road and many of them had chairs and benches outside in front of their windows, and almost all had window boxes or pots of plants. It was all very

40

clean and orderly and the people obviously take a pride in their homes.

Leaving Harderwijk the next morning it was not hard to eschew the delights of the Dolphinarium. It would have been very sad to see those beautiful creatures in captivity no matter how happy they seemed. Before leaving we took on fuel. Even doing small things like this took on momentous proportions because we were not sure how the boat would handle and had not yet established a routine with ropes and fenders, but we managed it without mishap.

There had been a motorboat moored on the fuel quay overnight and we had expected him to move off that morning. When he did not it became obvious we would just have to squeeze in on the end. The problem with that was that lots of other boats also wanted fuel and there was nowhere to moor whilst waiting. Every time there was a gap another boat arrived to take it. After a frustrating hour or so waiting for our chance to cast off and motor across we did what we should have done earlier and motored up and down just off the fuel berth and moved in when opportunity arose.

John was much happier once we had a full fuel tank, although he would have been even happier if he could have found a way to fill both of our fuel tanks. This was another problem we had. There were two tanks and the port tank had no filler hole and it was only connected to the starboard tank through the engine. It took a long time for the fuel to make its way into this auxiliary tank and so it was impossible to fill it to the top. It once had an opening in the top but this had been blocked off and John did not have the tools to remove the plug. The inability to fill this tank became something of an obsession with him. Whilst fuel was readily available in Holland, it was not so easy to obtain in France and when there we would need to be able to carry the maximum amount

Our chart showed a lock and a lifting bridge separating Harderwijk from the next section of the Randmeren. But whilst we had been there looking at possible boats to buy we had stayed at a hotel close by, at Hardersluis, and seen the work on a new road and tunnel. The main road was now diverted through this tunnel under the aqueduct so that no opening bridge was necessary. There was no longer a lock either and whilst we were dithering about which channel to take to go under the bridge another motorboat overtook us and we followed him through the gap.

We motored north in company with lots of other boats, heading for Ketelmere 35 km. away. We were surprised to find that the waterway was very wide and at places along the edge there were beaches and holiday bungalows. It was a lovely day and people were sunbathing and swimming. Several islands were dotted about and the larger ones had small harbours where one could tie up and small 'creeks' where pontoons were provided for boats. We found these were marked on the map as *aanlegplaatz* so that was another bit of learning for us. These were temporary mooring places but there was a charge levied, unlike in France where it was usually possible to tie up alongside the bank for free.

We encountered our first opening bridge and watched carefully to see what the other boats were doing. As we approached we saw that there was a span high enough for us to pass under without needing to wait for the main span to lift. Only yachts with high masts needed to wait until the road traffic was halted and the bridge lifted. At the next bridge there was also a lock, and we did not realise this until we were quite close. We saw the other boats tying up and I quickly rushed to hang the fenders out and ready the ropes. My heart began to beat faster as we approached and I quickly looped my rope ready to throw it over a bollard. I did not want the boat to be blown away from the quay by the wind before we were tied up, nor to miss lassoing the bollard and look like an amateur. I need not have worried; it was an anti-climax as the water only dropped about 30 cm. and the lock was very gentle. We almost did not need lines.

This lock marked the beginning of Ketelmere and from there we motored into the mouth of the river IJssel. This was quite exciting; we were now beginning to feel that our journey had started. There was still a long trek to go but we were moving south now and on the way. By 16.00 hrs we were in sight of Kampen, a succession of towers and spires along the river with a handsome bridge, the four towers of which were topped by gilded wheels.

We found a place in a harbour just across the river from the town. The harbour was in a small lake and very sheltered.

This was our first attempt at tying up in a marina since we had left Nulde and we motored in looking for a suitable place. We were hailed by a chap from the quay by the club house and directed into a berth like the one *Liberty* had been in at Nulde, with pilings. After two attempts we managed to squeeze in alongside a very smart new motorboat. The wind was quite strong and John had a little difficulty aiming *Liberty* between the pilings but the owners of the motorboat helped us and a chap whom we later discovered was the harbourmaster took our lines.

The people were very friendly. A small crowd were drinking at tables in the sunshine outside the clubhouse. It was a hot day and we decided to join them. We found that several of them spoke excellent English and were not afraid to chat to us. But we were feeling a little paranoid because when we approached initially we had heard a loud gust of laughter from this crowd. It was the same sort of situation that arises as when you go into a shop in Wales and the people inside are speaking Welsh. You assume they are talking about you when all they are doing is discussing the weather. On this occasion I assumed some joke had been made at the expense of the English. However another boat came in later and the same thing happened. The guffaws were because the harbourmaster had to haul himself from his chair and leave his beer once more to bring the boat in, and others in turn were helping him so they too were being laughed at.

We began to learn the protocol for coming into these harbours as we sat outside the club house with our drinks. We watched visitors approach the quay, which has obviously been designated as the visitors' quay. The harbourmaster directed them to a space and then helped them in.

The harbourmaster told us that he used to be an English teacher and this job was his retirement occupation. There was also a very friendly young woman who told us she managed the call centre for the ANWB. She also told us that they had recently had a visit by a team from the British AA which she had to conduct entirely in English.

The temperature had really soared today, which made a change from the rain we had been experiencing. We were glad of our cold beers. Two small children in life jackets were jumping into the water by the quay and swimming with their parents. It looked so refreshing that I decided to join them before supper. I went back to the boat and searched for my bathing suit which I knew I had brought. I turned out all the lockers, getting hotter and sweatier in the process. Eventually I decided to give up the search but not the swim. I had a pair of nylon shorts and a brief sun-top. They might not have been the most elegant garments and I may have looked a strange figure in turquoise shorts and orange top but they served the purpose and I climbed down our stern ladder, lowered myself into the deliciously cold water and I could almost hear my skin sizzle. The swim restored my energy and I felt ready to tackle the task of cooking a meal.

Lowering our inflatable dinghy into the water the following morning we used it to cross the river to the town for sight seeing and more shopping. We left the dinghy in a small harbour where the harbourmaster promised to keep an eye on it providing we returned before the evening influx of boats. Along the quay we found a large chandlery where there was everything from brass screws to folding bikes – a paradise for boat owners like us who were still equipping a boat. We were able to get those things we had not found in Harderwijk. We bought a flagstaff, a water carrier, a fuel can and sundry purchases and left them at the shop to be collected later. We then made our way to the tourist office where they gave us a leaflet recommending a walk round the town which we decided to follow. Kampen was on the estuary of the river IJssel and once was a moated town with its own fleet of ships. It was in its prime between 1330 and 1450 and became one of the later members of the Hanseatic trading league in 1440, growing rich from its trade with England and the Baltic. The Hanseatic League was formed by groups of merchants who sold the same type of wares within a city. They banded together to form a "hansa" and joined forces with those in other cities to form a "hanse". This league lasted for four centuries before losing its significance when the Far East and the United States entered the market. The town's prosperity has now increased again since the land reclamation of the Noord-Oostpolder and Flevoland.

The walk took us around the town and we admired the old buildings and churches including the old warehouses used by the "hansa" and we discovered the location of the old town gates. We passed the old town hall with statues carved on the outside, and a building still called the new tower although it was completed in the 14th century. Legend has it that lightning destroyed the top of the tower and grass began to grow on the remaining stump. Ever careful to use their resources local farmers asked if they could graze their cattle up there. It is said that a cow was hauled to the top but died on the way up. To commemorate this stupid request a cow has been hoisted to the top of the tower every year since, although now it has been replaced by a model, probably the one now standing in the town square.

The town used to be surrounded by a wall and 20 gates only three of which are left. We walked through one of them to a building that was once a Jewish Synagogue on the river front, and which reminded us poignantly of the atrocities of the last war when the Jewish community were deported during the night of 17 to 18 November 1942. This lovely building was now an exhibition centre, but has a memorial on the façade.

A restored sailing ship, the *De Kanze Kogge* was tied up at the quay. It is a replica of a wrecked medieval ship of the type used to transport goods to other Hanseatic towns – which thus played an important role in the history of Kampen. This boat is available for sailing trips.

We admired the bridge spanning the river; the huge gilded wheels are part of the lifting mechanism and glinted in the sunlight. We would be able to pass beneath without the bridge needing to lift for us.

After lunch at a brasserie and some more shopping we returned to collect our chandlery, loading it into our dinghy and returned to the boat. I decided it was warm enough for another short swim and afterwards I sunbathed on the deck, book in hand. I was running out of reading matter as I am an avid reader. We had bought some English books in Amsterdam but they would not last long. I hoped I would be able to exchange them with other English speaking boat owners as we travelled along.

We set off the next morning and planned to tie up at the town quay as we passed the town. The water container we had bought had a leak and we wanted to exchange it. But the quay was too high for *Liberty* and was blocked off by road works. We would just have to manage. We needed the water container because it was impossible to see inside our water tank and we did not know when it was last cleaned out. We dared not drink the tank water. We planned to fill this container from the mains tap at each marina. We thought we might still be able to use it if we did not fill it above the point of the leak, and until we could clean out the tanks this is what we did.

Chapter 4, - Deeper into Holland

Gaining experience

The weather continued to be hot and sunny. The temperatures reached 35 deg. C. and we had difficulty keeping cool, although it was not too bad when we were moving as our motion created a wind which cooled us down. What a change from the weather that we had experienced earlier in the trip. I unearthed  both of the sun umbrellas that were part of our equipment and fixed the lower part of them to the stanchions on deck with cable ties. When we needed them we slotted the top part in. On our first day out from Kampen we were able to motor with a sunshade up all day. That felt really delightful, sitting on deck, helming the boat, in sun top and shorts, beneath the shade of a parasol. There were no locks so we were able to relax for most of the day.

When a windmill came into view we shouted "Molen, molen" excitedly. It was easy to forget that the windmills are functional architecture. They stand exposed to the elements in the flat countryside where they can catch the wind, and add a very picturesque touch to otherwise unremarkable landscape.

But there was a lot of traffic – huge barges laden and un-laden, motorboats and yachts. Groynes had been built out into the main channel to increase the current and maintain the depth. On the Rhone, in France, these groynes, which serve the same purpose, were underwater and marked by a red or green marker buoy. Here they were made of stone and built out as part of the countryside. They often had trees growing on them. The result was a series of small bays where boats could pull out of the main stream for a lunch stop or fishing, and where cows could come to the water to drink.

We travelled to Deventer a journey of about 30 km and found a marina in another small lake off the main channel. This time we tied up under a huge sign which said 'Visitors' and I went in search of the harbourmaster. He directed us into a berth, this time on pontoon moorings which we were more used to.

At the far side of the lake was a sandy beach where families and dogs were swimming and frolicking. It looked very inviting on such a hot day. Once we were tied up we took our dinghy across for a swim. We had hoped it would be cleaner across the lake away from the boats but it was not so. The water resembled the thick pea soup which is a Dutch delicacy. It is inevitable that boats will discharge some diesel into the water, and ducks and dogs do what comes naturally, not to mention the human beings. We had a quick dip making sure to keep our heads above water, and returned to the boat. This was when an in-board shower would have been welcome. But we had a battery operated pump shower and with a bucket of clean water on deck we were able to use that to clean ourselves off.

Deventer was another ancient town and was also part of the Hanseatic League; in fact it still calls itself a Hanseatic town. But it was too far to visit without transport so we planned to move on the next day.

Leaving Deventer we swung out into the main channel and were immediately amazed by the force of the current. It was probably about 4 knots (5 mph) and flowing against us. But the countryside was pleasantly green and fertile and dotted with the occasional windmill.

Our next stopping place was Giesbeek, about 20 km. north of Arnhem. On the chart we found several marinas marked at various points in a very large meandering lake. The lake was probably as big as Lake Windermere and perfect for dinghies, and larger boats, we even saw a peniche (a large barge) anchored in there. There were several islands creating inlets and 'secret' nooks and crannies.

We made our way into the lake well away from the main river and meandered round the back of an island to find a large marina where we pulled onto the visitors' pontoon. It was a long walk from there to the harbour office where all the facilities were housed and which was up a steep ramp. We were given a numbered berth quite close to the office and then needed to walk back to the boat to bring her to the indicated berth. This was John's first experience of handling *Liberty* in a confined space and he was very nervous. Reversing was tricky because *Liberty* does not follow the rudder astern and tends to veer away. In the slight wind we were not sure how she would react. But he managed it, skirting round a coot's nest which was built on the end of one of the pontoons.

I was delighted to find a washing machine and dryer amongst the facilities and soon had my bundle of washing going round and round in there. It took two hours to wash, and one hour to dry, how very un-green. I was exhausted when it had finally finished as I had to walk up the steep ramp to put it in, back to the boat, up again to assess its state of readiness, and again to transfer it to the dryer, and finally to collect it when it was finished. It was very clean after all that washing and I was several pounds lighter.

But we were quickly learning that the Dutch have things well organised when it comes to facilities for boating. There was no wonder our boat did not have a shower. There was no need for one as the marinas have showers, and there were plenty of marinas. However such was the demand on the showers here that we had to use the disabled facilities, which were nice and roomy with space to dress in private. We were careful to make sure there were no disabled people likely to need them just then. The demand on the showers came mainly from hordes of youngsters who had just brought a fleet of dinghies in from the lake where they had been being taught to sail.

We decided to have some time off the next day and do absolutely nothing all morning which allowed us to recuperate from the heat and the stress of travelling. We placed deck chairs on the upper deck and sat under the parasols until after lunch, cool drinks at our sides. Unfortunately we were running low on some foods, particularly bread and fresh milk so we had to stir ourselves and find a shop before the end of the day. The harbourmaster directed us to the nearby village. We walked right around the marina and discovered a Spar supermarket in the body of an old windmill. This was a shopping first for us. I wandered around as if in a dream admiring the way the inside had been converted. I felt as though I was in a fairytale.

Getting there and taking the stuff back would have been much easier with our bikes – oh how we missed them. We had naturally added a bottle of wine and some cans of beer to our milk and bread and the shopping bags were very heavy on the way back. But I did not regret the extra litre of white wine, which we chilled in the fridge and drank with our evening meal.

A Dutch family pulled in alongside us later and engaged us in conversation. The whole family spoke excellent English including the children who were in their early teens. The parents were both teachers and were on holiday accompanied by the wife's parents, who were in another boat not dissimilar to ours. The grand-parents were new to boating and needed to be helped in and out of their mooring place. We told them that we too were new to motor-boating and the next morning they insisted in helping us out of our berth and round the corner into the fuel berth. The fuel in our tanks had now made a level and we could put more fuel in the starboard tank.

We have found that all the fuel berths in the Dutch marinas are in inaccessible places. I suppose they need to be near the road to make them accessible for the fuel tankers. But we had a tricky corner to negotiate and the wind was quite strong. We were very grateful for the help. It was an unusual experience for us to be the novices, and I am afraid we removed another little bit of paint from our hull as we caught the corner of the pontoon.

We made our way now to Arnhem which is the capital of Gelderland, and only 2 hrs away. The current was becoming even stronger; soon we would be in the river Rhine. Just the sound of that name filled me with apprehension as I have stood on its banks in Germany and seen the huge commercial boats plying up and down against a fierce current. But the reality was less frightening and certainly less intimidating than the river Mersey where we have sailed regularly.

There were lots of commercial boats and much traffic generally. At one point we met (head on) a motorboat that had crossed to our side of the river to overtake two other boats, and seemed to think that we should pull into mid-stream to accommodate him. We soon disabused him of this but the encounter shook John quite considerably. Horns were blown and fists shaken. I was glad we were only doing a short trip as it was stressful enough getting used to how this new boat handles without having to cope with incidents such as this.

We reached our intended marina after turning north from the IJssel into the Lower Rhine. There was a rowing club at river level and the office and restaurant were on the floor above, with a restaurant and balcony overlooking the river.

The marina was quite full when we arrived and we were directed into a rather narrow space alongside the rowing club. The wind was quite strong and despite willing hands to help us we caught our hull on the corner of one of the pontoons. It was quite sharp and made a long scratch on the hull, the worst so far. One of the harbour staff appeared soon afterwards with a fender which he tied over the offending projection, making jokes about locking the stable door after the horse has bolted.

The marina was at the mouth of a long 'cut' which housed several factories and an oil refinery. Huge barges and tankers passed continually, within feet of our stern, and we were bounced about by their wash. It was not the most restful place to be but was handy for the shops and the town. We could also see the traffic passing on the Lower Rhine on its way to and from Rotterdam - barges, hotel boats and container ships.

Circumstances conspired to keep us in Arnhem for several days and we were quite glad about that as it provided us with an opportunity for some more sightseeing and to do more jobs on the boat.

Close to the marina we found an 'out of town' shopping area within 10 mins walking distance and were able to use this to keep our store cupboards replenished. There were Lidl and Jumbo supermarkets as well as Halfords, a hardware store and an off-licence. But again none of them could accept either our Debit or our Credit Card. Before we could do much shopping there we needed to go into Arnhem itself and get some cash.

I was looking forward to visiting Arnhem it was somewhere I had always longed to see and I wondered if it would live up to my expectations. The town was once a wealthy resort, a watering-hole to which the rich merchants of Amsterdam and Rotterdam would flock to idle away their fortunes. Last century it became better known as the place where thousands of British and Polish troops died in the failed Allied airborne operation of September 1944, code-named Operation Market Garden. Now the visitors are largely the British who flock there to pay their respects to the soldiers who died, and to visit the battle sites.

The harbourmaster at our marina was a friendly chap with a dark, short beard, and a navy fishermen's sweater and cap. But he did not speak a lot of English. John asked him how to get into Arnhem, hoping there would be a bus and we were directed along a road which he said went to the station and which turned out to be a dead end. On reflection he probably meant bus stop when he said station because the train station was a long way on the other side of town. Returning to the main road we walked into town alongside the river. It took us about 20 minutes and we passed several bus stops but the only buses we saw were going in the opposite direction. But there obviously were buses and we made a note of the number for our return.

Our first priority was the cash machine which we found in the main square near the *Eusebiuskerk*, a huge sixteenth century church which was almost totally destroyed during the war and had been beautifully restored and extensively renovated for the fiftieth anniversary of Operation Market Garden in 1994.

We next collected leaflets and information about the places we wanted to visit from the tourist office in the centre of town.

First on our list was a visit to the Airborne Museum, commemorating the battle of Arnhem. The museum was not in Arnhem but in Oosterbeek a few miles out of town. However we now had good information and took the bus.

The museum was in the former headquarters of Major-General Urquhart, the British Divisional Commander at the Battle. We were able to see actual film footage of the conflict, look at equipment, arms and ammunition dug up after the end of the war, and to see very realistic dioramas of scenes from the battle. We were able to follow the events from the air landings, the march to the bridge, and the fierce fighting in Arnhem and Oosterbeek, to the crossing of the river. All of this was commemorated in the film, A Bridge Too Far.

The plan had been to parachute three airborne Divisions behind enemy lines, each responsible for taking and holding particular bridgeheads until the army could force their way north to join them. Field Marshal Montgomery wanted to speed the advance of the Allies through Holland and into the Ruhr, around the back of the Siegfried line, in order to end the war early, as much of France, and all of Belgium had already been liberated. The American Airborne Division which landed at Nijmegen to secure the crossing of the River Waal was successful, but the landings around Arnhem ran into serious problems: there were far more opposing troops than had been anticipated. The 2nd Parachute Battalion, under Lieutenant-Colonel John Frost, did manage to capture the north end of the road bridge across the Rhine, but it proved impossible to capture the southern end. Extraordinary heroism was shown and they held their position for four days. Meanwhile other Polish and British battalions had concentrated around the bridgehead at Oosterbeek, which they held at tremendous cost under General Urquhart but it became apparent that reinforcements would not be able to get through and a dramatic withdrawal saved 2163 soldiers from an original force of 10,005.

For me the most poignant thing was a commemorative plaque by the gateway put there in 1994 honouring the people of Arnhem and thanking them for their sacrifice during the battle. All the townspeople were forced to abandon their homes and were not able to return until 1945 when the peace treaty was signed. Most of them had to live in nearby woods. I had a lump form in my throat when I read this, which got bigger as we toured the museum. During the battle many hundreds of thousands of Dutch people suffered from hunger, cold and fear and many of them perished. The Germans plundered their homes, and their household goods were transported to Germany. Arnhem, Oosterbeek and other villages remained 'ghost-towns' until the liberation by the Allies. Holland had suffered five years of occupation.

It was all very moving. John and I were overcome to the point of silence and were full of compassion. When we had seen all we wanted to see we sat on a bench in the garden, holding hands, and recovering ourselves.

Rather soberly we made our way back to the boat, this time taking the bus all the way.

On another visit to Arnhem we visited the *Openluchtmuseum* (Open Air Museum) on the outskirts of town. To get there we caught the bus and were surprised to find it on a hill. We did not think there were any hills in Holland. Later I learned that this was one of the spots where glaciers had pushed up hilly ridges in the terrain.

It was on a magnificent site where over 80 ancient houses and farms from different parts of the country had been re-erected to preserve a picture of the daily life of ordinary people in the country as it was in the past and had developed in the course of time. This was of great interest to me as the modern Netherlands were very different from what I had expected. I had a picture in my mind of a country of windmills, cheese, Delftware, bicycles, dykes and tulips, where the men wore baggy trousers and clogs and the women wore starched caps and voluminous skirts. I was eager to visit the country of my imagination at last.

The site covers 110 acres and a historic tramline had been re-built to transport visitors around the park, and the tram depot from Arnhem, which was bombed during the war, had been re-erected there. We were grateful to be able to hop on and off the tram as we visited the various parts of the museum. Where possible the buildings had been placed in groups that resembled the traditional villages of the different regions of Holland – from the farmsteads of Friesland to the farming communities of South Holland and the peat colonies of Drenthe. I particularly enjoyed the North Holland section, which contained a combination of rural, urban and fishing cultures around a small waterway with a traditional Dutch lifting bridge.

We ate a picnic beside a windmill overlooking a children's playground where an old-style carousel played organ music as it whirled the brightly coloured and gilded horses up and down on barley-sugar poles. We had a drink at the Hanekamp Inn, from Zwolle, dating from 1708. Travellers once outspanned their horses here on their way to and from the cattle markets where they would complete their business and then spend the night. This inn was also a headquarters for the Cossacks who came to Zwolle when the country was liberated from the French in 1813.

There were several working craftshops and factories, demonstrating the traditional skills of papermaking, milling, baking, cheese-making, brewing and bleaching.

We visited buildings ranging from an eel-peddler's shack with an earth floor and containing nothing more than a bed and which was condemned in 1918 as being unfit for human habitation, to a Merchant's House from Koog aan de Zaan. The Merchant's house was U-shaped and built in 1686-87. It consisted five different parts which were filled with period furniture, and which had an ornamental garden running down to the water's edge. I was intrigued to see, in some of the farmhouses, traditional box beds which were built into cupboards and which extended backwards into the barn where they were surrounded by hay to keep them warm.

We could have spent several days here but time and energy were running out. However we made sure we had time at the end to look at the extensive display of regional costumes in the basement and were surprised to discover how recently many of them were worn for everyday occasions, in fact some of the elderly women in North Holland still wear them.

As we made our way back to the marina we both agreed that it had been a fascinating, entertaining and informative day. John had enjoyed it as much as I had, and this was a man who was not keen on sight seeing.

As usual on our return to the boat we would make ourselves a cup of tea and chill out on the after deck if weather allowed. The deck was almost at a level with the balcony of the harbour office, which was also the bar and we were able to make eye contact with the customers. A group of them smiled down on us and I raised my cup and said "English tea", in reply one of the men raised a glass and said "Dutchish beer!"

We had arranged for some post to be delivered to us from England. We were waiting for a mail order delivery of a herbal supplement which John takes for his arthritis and as this had not yet arrived we filled in the time doing jobs around the boat, including rubbing down and painting that scratch on the hull.

We found a branch of Gamma (pronounced Hammer) a DIY store, just across the road on a new industrial estate. John bought an electric drill and a jigsaw and was busy fitting a log and depth sounder to the instrument panel. We only had basic tools on board because of the weight restrictions on our luggage and as a handyman John was finding this frustrating. He also bought a large spanner with which to try to remove the plug in the top of the port fuel tank, but it was not strong enough.

The nearness of the Gamma DIY store was a great help in assisting us to do several small jobs. Hooks went up inside cupboards and handles were screwed where handholds were needed. We even spent some time removing flaking paint from the back deck and touching it up.

I re-glued some headlining over one of the lockers which was coming unstuck in the heat. To my great delight I discovered a lifestyle shop in the shopping centre and bought some acrylic tumblers and a range of gingham-lined plastic baskets into which I organised our clothes. This made them easier to reach in the lockers.

There were lots of other jobs which we wanted to do and which had become evident as we used the boat. The steering was very stiff and we were wondering if it might be possible to fit hydraulic steering at the end of the season. There was also a shower to fit. We had thought it would be easy to fit one into the spare cabin in place of the second toilet but this was not looking so feasible now. We would need to think again.

The sunshades were a boon but had to be folded down when we went through locks; they would therefore be a nuisance in the French canals and would need replacing with a bimini (a permanent folding sun canopy). We were regarding this as a shake-down cruise and were planning to tackle the larger jobs at the end of the season.

The weather was like nothing we had experienced in England. We were used to the rain but it was usually consistent and cold. Here it would rain for days on end then stop by lunchtime after which the sun would come out and soon we would be expiring with the heat. One morning we woke to find there was a very strong wind, Force 5. We were glad to be able to stay here and enjoy the facilities of the town until the wind abated. Better weather was apparently on the way.

We waited several days for our parcel. The harbourmaster was very kind and phoned the sorting office, and even sent one of his staff to try to find it but to no avail. We even made the trip ourselves so as not to bother the harbourmaster again. We were wondering whether it had been 1) impounded by Dutch customs, or 2) held up by the bombing in London which must have disrupted a number of services. Fortunately we had found a herbalist in the station complex in Amsterdam and bought some of the tablets for him there so we can manage, but it was puzzling, and we never did find out why it was not delivered.

The only thing we really missed here was the companionship of other English speakers. The Dutch people would pass the time of day with us, and exchange pleasantries, but did not chat or invite us onto their boats as British people would. I expected this would change when we got into France.

We would sit on the deck and watch the other boats come in. They were almost all Dutch but one day we got quite excited when an English boat moored alongside us. Oh, good, we thought we can exchange information and perhaps swap some books. Once they were settled we walked round to say 'Hi'. The husband came out on deck to talk to us and was quite friendly in a slightly embarrassed way, but his wife stayed in the cabin and smiled at us through the window like the Mona Lisa. It was obvious we weren't going to be invited aboard and when we suggested a drink later it did not receive an enthusiastic response. We went back to our boat and pondered on this. We were used to extreme friendliness in the sailing fraternity. In Greece we would always approach or be approached by fellow nationals in the same harbour, which usually resulted in an invite for coffee or G & Ts., and some good friendships have resulted. In Holland this was the third English boat we had seen and none of them had wanted to socialise. In this case we decided that the wife was probably a minor celebrity and they were holidaying in Holland where she was least likely to be recognised and bothered by her fans. Perhaps she was an actress on Coronation Street or East Enders? The following morning when they came out on deck to prepare for departure I got a good look at her and she was certainly not someone I had seen before, and she did not act or look like a celebrity. They exchanged a few more words before departing. We decided that they were just unsociable.

Another day a neat little German motor sailor arrived. The husband helmed the boat close to the harbour office. People were on the balcony with drinks but there was no sign of the harbourmaster. There were various ways of attracting his attention. Most boats shouted or whistled; some got out their mobile phones and called the number painted on the outside of the building. The woman on this boat was looking hopefully at the people on the balcony and as we were close by I suggested that she shout. She grinned back at me and did so with the intended result. I met her again in the shower room and she asked me questions about the use of the showers and about shops and buses, in halting English.

That evening we ate in the clubhouse as I had decided it was too hot to cook on board. We were sitting outside overlooking the river sipping cold beers when the German couple came in and we invited them to join us - strangers in a strange land, banding together for companionship. We passed an interesting hour or two exchanging information. John speaks a little German having spent his National Service on the Rhine. They came from Dusseldorf and had negotiated the Rhine to reach Holland, something which they do every year. Perhaps I am unnecessarily worried about the Rhine.

Their boat was a 29 ft. fibreglass yacht built to simulate an older wooden boat and with its varnished coach roof looked very authentic. Inevitably the rain began again just as we had finished eating and we parted company.

We finally 'dug up our roots' or more appropriately cast off our lines at 11.45 on Friday, 29th July. We had waited for yet another post which did not deliver our parcel but now we were on our way. First we motored back into Arnhem where a bunker boat dispensed fuel right by the famous bridge. This plain modern bridge had been rebuilt and renamed the John Frostbrug (the John Frost Bridge) after the commander of the battalion that defended it for four days. It remains a symbol of people's remembrance of the battle, and on one of our walks into the town we had stopped to look at the concrete plinths bearing photographs of battle scenes, which were erected on a raised area at one end of the bridge.

At the bunker boat we found not only fuel but a floating chandlery and we were able to get a bottle of gas as well. This was another bit of learning for us as these bunker boats were moored in a permanent place and were marked on the chart. Now we knew where we could get fuel and chandlery.

I'm sure we could have spent many a happy hour in the chandlery, but John had the engine running and the wheel in his hands and we were off.

Sadly we left yet another layer of paint on the bunker boat as the current gripped us just as we were tying up and swung the stern out into the stream, the result was that we came alongside to port instead of to starboard and I had no fenders on that side. Another little something learned – fenders both sides. But it was only paint – it can be touched up. *Liberty* was a good strong boat.

Chapter 5 - On our way again

With Trepidation

We moved from the NederRijn into the Pannerdensksanaal – in reality the same river which had been canalised. This canal connects the upper and lower Rhineland.

The commercial traffic was constant, mainly peniches but also hotel boats taking tourists up the Rhine. The *Prins Willem Alexander*, the cause of our anxiety in Harderwijk, passed us. It was a hotel boat and was registered in Harderwijk so I guess it spends the winter there. I am glad it did not arrive whilst we were there. It was enormous. As it passed us it seemed to go on for ever.

The water was choppy and we were bounced about a bit, not just from the wind which whipped up the surface of the water but from the washes of the other boats. Poor *Liberty* was tossed every which way.

For the first time we experimented with changing over the steering position whilst we were under way. John went below and I remained at the outside position. I throttled back, took the engine out of gear and John reversed the procedure. It worked smoothly and he was delighted with how easily the boat handled from inside. I took over the steering to give him a break and increase my confidence but immediately regretted it. The river was wide at this point and I was cruising well out from the side when we were overtaken by a fast motorboat to port and at the same time a speedboat decided to cut in to starboard. *Liberty* was caught in the wash from both boats and tossed first to one side and then to the other, like a bucking bronco. John, who was in the cabin, was wondering what was going on as all the cupboard doors burst open, bottles and jars shot out onto the floor. The kettle fell off the cooker – it was full of water. Our pottery figure of Cap'n Bob fell off the helm position and down the cabin stairs, breaking off his head. I hoped it would mend. I kept closer into the side after that.

We turned into the river Waal after 10 km. moving now in a westerly direction until we came to the entrance to the Maas-Waalkanaal. By this time the sunny weather had deserted us and rain was coming down very heavily. What a time to encounter a major challenge such as a huge lock, amidst several large boats intent on going about their business, dwarfing our little pleasure boat. Several container boats were exiting from the lock and we cowered into the side. We wondered how to proceed. The lock's radio channel (18) was given on the chart and I used the ship's radio to ask rather nervously if it was in order for us to use the lock. Receiving permission we followed a peniche into a lock the size of a cathedral, where dark and dripping walls towered above us and were urged to move right to the front by the lady lockkeeper, and then by the crew of the peniche who invited us to tie alongside them. What a relief. I had been trying to get a line onto bollards set into the slimy wall but the bollards were not directly underneath each other and I was wondering how I would transfer our lines from one to the other as the lock filled and we went up. We tied on our lines and rose together with the peniche until the lock was level with the canal above. When the lock gates were opened they urged us to leave first and move out into the canal. We were glad to be out; we were not looking forward to negotiating these large locks in the commercial part of Holland and Belgium.

This was altogether a miserable trip. We had moved to the outside helm position to negotiate the lock – John has to be outside to help with the lines and also to see more clearly what he is doing. Visibility was reduced and we could really do with windscreen wipers for our spectacles. We pulled the peaks of our baseball caps as low down over our eyes as we could to keep off the driving rain. But the canal was straightforward and there was not much traffic.

After another 14 km. travelling we reached the lock at the other end of the canal. This was not in use as a lock at this time as its purpose was mainly to prevent flooding, but traffic was restricted to one-way passage through. As we approached we could see that there were red and green lights, simultaneously, and wondered which one to believe. There was a peniche ahead of us which pulled alongside a short quay and two or three pleasure boats slowed down also. We spotted a sign which explained in four languages that when we had red and green lights together we must wait. Sure enough a tiny motorboat emerged from the opposite direction and when he had cleared the lock we were all allowed through. The peniche took precedence as was its right as a working vessel. Although we have found that many of the peniche skippers will allow the smaller faster traffic to go first, this one did not.

The rain had cleared by the time we were looking for a mooring for the night, close to Mook in Limburg. We were now in Holland's southernmost province, a finger of land that pushes down into Belgium.

After passing the village we turned into an attenuated lake, the Mookerplas where several harbours were located. This is part of a large recreational area where lakes have been created from chalk pits.

The first small harbour at the entrance to the lake had pontoons which were only big enough for small boats. We passed them and proceeded into the lake and found mooring areas running along the shore with posts for mooring but no quay. There was another harbour through a narrow bridge. Several yachts were moored by the shore and had used the Mediterranean method – dropping a stern anchor and approaching the shore to where they took lines from their bow to the posts. We decided to join them. We did not have a stern anchor but dropped the bow anchor and John climbed into the dinghy to take a stern rope ashore. Being a man-made lake the sides were sloping, and were concrete below the vegetation, and getting ashore was not easy. He got his feet wet and got nettled in the process. *Liberty* had only been provided with short lines for mooring and even when we tied two together we found that we were so close to the edge that our rudder was hitting the concrete. I made a note to buy, or bring from home, some longer lines.

We decided to free anchor a little way off shore but were uncertain of the depth. John improvised a depth sounder with a 10 lb. hammer and a length of knotted rope. It turned out to be only 3 metres deep and we were able to lay our anchor successfully. We had bought a depth sounder and John had put the instrument on our helm position but we needed to have *Liberty* lifted out of the water before we could finalise it.

We were now a little way off shore and able to appreciate our surroundings. We had countryside with fields of cows close to where we were anchored but on the other side of the lake and extending round the bottom was a huge caravan site.

I counted over 200 caravans and those were just the ones I could see. Many of them had small boats moored at the water's edge close to them and several boats were zooming about. The phrase "angry wasps" came to mind. The rain had ceased and one or two wind surfers came out to enjoy the late afternoon sunshine, together with some water skiers. I can see the point of using a motorboat for towing water skiers but most of the boats here were just buzzing about for the sheer hell of it and spoiling the otherwise tranquil evening for the rest of us.

Despite that we enjoyed our evening meal and a glass of wine on the upper deck, under sun umbrellas watching the sun set over the entrance to the lake, silhouetting the trees in shades of apricot and burnt umber. It lasted several minutes and I watched with delight before it faded and left the world to the gathering dusk, and the sound of a distant bingo caller from the caravan site.

A sign on the bank indicated that mooring here would cost 70 cents per metre, per night, and we had hoped that this did not apply to anchored boats. We hoped in vain. As night fell a pleasant, elderly gentleman in a motorboat came along and extracted a fee of 8.40€ from us. That was almost as much as we had paid at the harbour the night before where we had had full facilities. I suppose they have to cover the cost of draining the polders and dredging the lakes and canals somehow. And of course he had disappeared by the time we worked out that we had been overcharged.

It rained solidly all night but had cleared up as we left the following morning and the sun started to peek through a gap in the grey cloud overhead. Other boats were beginning to emerge from the harbour under the bridge and we joined a convoy heading for the Maas. We were the only boat to turn south. Most of these other boats were Germans, heading for the Rhine in the north, which was not surprising as we were very close to the German border.

We noticed several temporary mooring places marked on the chart, usually with the addendum that *overnaching* was *verboten*. We saw these points along the main river and they were quays or small harbours where we could tie up for shopping or sight seeing but not for overnight anchoring. If we were to come this way again we would bear these in mind.

After 14 kilometres we came to a huge lock, Sambeek. It was a double lock with two chambers side by side, 16 metres wide, 33 metres deep and 142 metres long. As we approached with our fenders in place, lines on each cleat and our hearts in our mouths John suggested that we should rename the boat *'Trepidation'* because that was what we were approaching the lock with.

There were several small boats travelling with us and we hung back purposely so that we could see what they would do and follow suit. They all went into the lock and tied up on the starboard side. We did the same and a minute or two later we saw a huge peniche approaching which joined us in the lock, tying up on the port side.

Again there were bollards set in the wall, but this time they were one above the other, and we were able to attach our lines, and as we moved up very smoothly it was easy to transfer them to the bollard above as we went. I concentrated very hard as I have a horror of taking a line off a bollard and not being able to get it onto the next bollard before the boat swings away from the lock wall.

Two small children with father and grandfather were watching the rise of the boats and enthusiastically greeting each one as they arrived. When we left they were at the gates shouting their 'Good-byes'.

The sun continued to shine as we made our way down the Maas. We passed several holiday sites where very smart bungalows lined the banks, each with its own motorboat or dinghy ramp. Some children were using inflatable canoes at the water's edge and we slowed down to reduce our wake. I think they found this a little disappointing as when I looked back they were enthusiastically pointing their boats at the waves to enjoy the thrill of being bounced about. They would have liked a stronger wash.

At another place we saw small plots of land, individually fenced, with concrete slipways, and a sign saying *Te Koop* – they were selling land for more holiday bungalows perhaps?

Another feature of the countryside in Holland was small ferries for bicycles or foot passengers, and sometimes

 for cars as well. There was so much water that ferries were needed to take passengers from one side of the canal to the other. Most were chain driven and accompanied by a couple of unmanned boats one of which carried a light and a solar panel to power it.

Dodging the ferry was always a little nail biting. We had to judge when it would be leaving and then decide whether to speed up and get past ahead of it or slow down and pass behind.

One or two yachts under sail were also using this waterway and provided another hazard to watch out for and give way to. Motor always gives way to sail.

We arrived on the outskirts of a town called Venlo at 14.30 where a yacht harbour shares an inlet with an industrial harbour. The wind was blowing quite strongly at this point and we were apprehensive about tying up in such conditions amongst moored boats but we had little choice. Fortunately the harbour was well sheltered by high grassy banks topped by a smart club house. It was also very up to date and provided us with another 'first'. As we turned into the entrance we saw an electronic sign board high above the first pontoon which said 'Welcome'. Thinking that this marked the visitors' pontoon we headed towards it to discover that the pontoon was thronged with boats. We turned into a narrow channel looking for a space and as I glanced back at the Welcome sign I saw that it now read S30. We were being directed to space No. 30 on pontoon S. How's that for technology? Luckily there was someone on the boat in number 31 as the space was very narrow. But with their help and John's improving motor boat skills we slipped in like a foot into a shoe.

I found a washing machine in the club house so I was able to get our bedding washed. But as at Guisebeek it involved several walks to the club house, first to get the washing in, then to transfer it to the dryer and finally to collect it at the end. This machine displayed the length of the wash programme on an electronic timer, which was very useful. But when I went up at the time the previous wash should have finished someone else was there before me, so I left my bundle in the 'queue'. I knew I would get very fit with all the walking.

Showers were free, hot and clean, there was a lovely restaurant and free bicycle hire. There was even a pump out facility for toilet holding tanks.

Sitting outside the harbourmaster's office was an elderly lady in a black skirt and green woolly jumper. She was knitting. At her side was a basket of knitted ducks, the body of each duck contained a bar of soap. I could not resist buying one to sit with my pottery ducks on a shelf in the boat. The proceeds were for charity.

This was another well equipped and secure boat facility. They had storage ashore for boats and the harbour was so pleasant that we had a discussion about the possibility of getting *Liberty* lifted out here so that we could do the little jobs which were needed, such as fitting the depth sounder. Whilst she was out of the water we could also take the train home for some of the equipment from our previous boat such as longer lines, bicycles, life jackets etc. Whilst we were pondering on this the following day we borrowed bikes from the harbourmaster and cycled into the town. Venlo is part of the combined city of Venlo/Blerick which began as a Roman settlement and later grew rich on trade in the Middle Ages. Very few buildings in the town survived World War II and it all seemed very modern with a pedestrianised town centre and brick-paved streets. John was apprehensive about cycling, particularly after an experience in France when he had fallen off his bike and scarred his nose. He hates cycling on the roads on (to us) the wrong side. But I persuaded him that there would be cycle tracks and there were. The tracks were completely separate from the road and we had no problem. We loaded our panniers with groceries and cycled back to the marina without event.

The towns in Holland all have a similar pattern. The roads are paved with brick and the houses are usually terraced, they are what we would call 'town houses', with well-tended front gardens and garden furniture. That evening we had a discussion about leaving *Liberty*, and spent another night there to sleep on it, eventually deciding that we ought to push on. We were quite a way from Amsterdam and it would probably not be practical.

We continued on to Maasbracht. The journey was uneventful apart from two locks as we entered and left the Kanaal Wessem-Nederweert. As we approached the final lock I could see that it was open but the lights were red. We were the only boat in sight so I radioed to the lockkeeper. He did not speak English and asked me if I spoke French. Foolishly I told him I did and asked to pass through the lock. He answered me in French but I had no idea what he was saying. However the lights turned green and we entered the lock, accompanied now by another motorboat which appeared at the last moment perhaps that was what he was telling me.

We had identified two possible harbours just off the entrance to the Juliana canal at Maasbracht. When we arrived it became obvious that both of them were boat building and repair yards with quite primitive facilities. But there were several boats tied up with spaces between so we headed in and tied up. Once in we could not find a harbourmaster or an office but we walked through one of the yards out onto the nearby road and found a signboard for the firm with a phone number on it. I called the number and the person on the other end said it will be OK to stay and he would contact the harbourmaster who turned out to be a Dutchman living on one of the boats. He spoke very little English but came to our boat after about an hour and charged us 5€ which included electricity. Apart from the fact that we had no view and the sound of engines from the nearby boat sheds disturbed the peace of the afternoon, we were well pleased with the price, especially as there was a small town nearby. Access to the road was through a large, weed-filled yard where two half completed peniches lay untended. All around us were boat sheds, boats in various states of disrepair and boats covered with tarpaulins for storage.

We walked along the road which eventually turned towards the river where we were amazed to see more peniches tied up, dozens of them. This was obviously a place where they wait for work, as well as where repairs were undertaken.

We found a wonderful chandlery and were able to get a Navicarte of Belgium, some longer warps, and a siphon pump for use with the spare diesel can. The chandlery was well laid out with ropes, brassware and with polished woodwork everywhere. We enjoyed poking around, and chatting to the shop owner who was a retired barge skipper. The Navicarte is a book containing a linear map of the Belgian canals with all the mooring places and facilities marked. We had obtained these for the French canals and found them invaluable.

From Maasbracht we made our way to Maastricht on the Dutch, German border. We had to negotiate locks at the beginning and towards the end of the Juliana canal but trepidation had been put to one side. We were now approaching the locks with confidence so we decided that perhaps we would not rename the boat.

The Juliana canal takes traffic to the west of the original river Maas, which forms the border with Belgium. It was built high above the countryside and it was possible to get glimpses of towns and villages, an occasional windmill, and huge sand and gravel quarries, down in the valley below.

The canals themselves were very uninteresting and only the sunshine turned a boring experience into a pleasant one. One little bit of anxiety was experienced when we reached a stretch where the canal curved to accommodate the path of the river alongside it, and passed under two bridges. It was very narrow and we saw a sign which said that passing oncoming traffic was not allowed, and gave a VHF channel number (10) to radio ahead. The canal was quite wide enough for us, even if we did meet a peniche. We concluded that the signs were meant for the peniches, which would need to give way to each other and probably stop in order to do so. Loaded peniches need to use the centre of the canal as they almost touch the bottom. We kept a listening watch on Channel 10 just in case.

Shortly after we came out of the narrow stretch we met an enormous peniche, very wide and fully loaded but here there was room to pass without much difficulty.

The old river joined us as we entered Maastricht. We considered going into the ancient harbour here, which was through another lock, but had set our sights on a new marina outside the town. On our way we passed several boats moored to the west side of a training wall which joins the piers of two bridges in mid-stream. This was another possible mooring place but we thought the security might be poor. This was a big town after all, with all its attendant problems.

We travelled on to St. Pieters' marina, named after some caves in the hillside further south. We were welcomed onto the visitor's quay at 14.00 hrs. The harbourmaster was still at lunch but a Dutch couple took our lines and helped us make fast. Once we were tied up we passed the time of day chatting to them.

The harbourmaster turned out to be a pleasant rotund fellow who spoke a little English. He booked us in, allocated space on a pontoon just opposite the visitors' quay and gave us an electronic key for the gate. The fees here were a little higher than we had paid before (14€) but showers and electricity were free, there was an open air swimming pool and a restaurant, as well as picnic tables on the riverside. The facilities were shared with a large camp site next door where full-sized fridges and cookers could be seen permanently installed in awnings adjoining the caravans.

Walking into the city the next day we were amazed to find a lovely ancient town, glimpsed only briefly as we passed yesterday. All its old buildings were beautifully preserved on one side of the river and the new town had developed across the bridge, St. Servaasbrug. This was an elegant 13th century bridge with seven semicircular arches and a modern section through which ships can pass.

I had not known what to expect from Maastricht. I had thought it would be a big modern city. It had made headlines in 1992 when John Major was prime minister of Britain and came here to sign the Maastricht Treaty. This treaty ratified the European Union, and the MECC Conference Centre in which the business was conducted was opposite our marina.

I was shamed by my ignorance. This is one of the oldest towns in Holland and a truly delightful old city. We bought a map from the tourist office, and decided to return at 12.30 for a guided tour in English. The tourist office is housed in the Dinghuis, a tall late 15th century building at the end of the main shopping street.

We had an early lunch, joining many other people at a café in Vritjthof Square where trees shaded the cobbles and the church of St. Servatius towered above us. Open air cafés are a large feature of Maastricht and it was wonderful to sit in one of them and watch the world go by. But we did not have time to sit for long as we had to hurry back to the tourist office for the guided tour which turned out to be fascinating. We walked for an hour and a half around the town. We learned that Maastricht was the first bishopric in the Netherlands and had been an impressive fortress. We were taken to see the medieval walls, a 13th century church that still has a Roman tower, part of the old church building, and a working water-mill where bread was still made. I could not resist holding our small party up whilst I bought a loaf of the deliciously crusty brown bread. We went inside St. Servaasbasiliek and admired the ancient architecture. The church dates from the second century but the earliest visible architecture was 11th century. In the treasury of the church is a magnificent restored reliquary containing the relics of St. Servatius and St. Martin of Tongeren. It is made of wood covered with embossed gilded copper plate in the shape of a house and it dates from about 1160.

The Romans settled in Maastricht in 50 BC because this was a place where the Maas could be crossed on foot and it became an important stop on their trade route from Cologne to the coast. This ford and its strategic position near the borders with Germany and Belgium and close to France, means that Maastricht has been fought over for many centuries. A plaque on the side of a building showed a lion and a wolf confronting each other across a lamb. The lamb represents Maastricht.

The name Maastricht derives from the words *Mosae Trajectum* or "Maas Crossing".

After our tour we did a little shopping and I bought a small oven/grill which I thought might be useful in the place of an oven on *Liberty*. Clothes were expensive here, and we walked down what our guide told us was the most expensive street in Europe where designer goods were on sale. Not for us - we just looked. There were more of the lifestyle shops here selling knick knacks; wicker baskets, candles, oil lamps and fancy kitchen ware, all attractively displayed. Delicatessens and bakeries offered a tempting aroma of food and I bought savoury pies to take back for tea.

As we would be leaving Holland after Maastricht I decided that I would take the opportunity to buy Dutch dolls for my grand-daughters. They were easy enough to find and I packed them carefully away.

We left the old town via the Helpoort gate, which dates from the early 13th century and also formed part of the early medieval fortifications. This is the oldest surviving town gate in Holland. It is now on the edge of an attractive park.

We were very impressed to be told that one of the main squares in Maastricht had been dug up recently and an underground car park constructed below it, after which the square was replaced exactly as it had been, complete with brick cobbles, and bronze carnival figures in one corner. These carnival figures were just slightly larger than life and were painted brightly in yellow, pink, blue and green. Our guide told us that before their removal they were plain bronze and that the citizens were amazed and not altogether pleased by the decision to paint them. It was difficult to tell that they were made of bronze now.

Back at the boat we found we had company in the form of a Dutchman who had moored his yacht alongside us. He told us that he had sailed across the North Sea, round Britain, into the Bay of Biscay and thence to the Mediterranean and back through the French canals. He had sailed single-handedly most of the time, although a friend had joined him for part of the trip.

We noticed that he had a Belgian flag and before he left the next day we negotiated the swapping of this for a packet of coffee and we were well pleased because we would need this when we moved into Belgium.

Chapter 6 –Belgium

With Confidence

We stayed in Maastricht a few days more. Even though it was now August the weather was very unsettled so it was an ideal opportunity for more sightseeing. The walk into Maastricht took about 15 minutes along the river.

We wandered down more narrow streets and alleyways and joined the citizens of the town at a pavement café, watching the world go by, and watching some street theatre performed by an international Christian group bringing 'The Word' to young people. They had a message, performed in mime and music, about the evils of drugs. It was interesting but I am not sure how effective it might have been.

We finally left on Monday 8th August, looking forward to reaching Liège in Belgium by the end of the day. We crossed the border immediately and after 2 km. stopped for a lock. There were several boats tied up to a long quay outside the lock, and a couple of boats milling about. They had the air of having been waiting some time so we decided to tie up. I chose not to call the lock, anticipating that one of the other boats, with better language skills, would already have done so. We tied up at 10.15. There was a road tanker plying up and down the quay and we remembered that we had been told that Dutch people often come down here across the border to buy diesel, which was cheaper in Belgium. After about 15 minutes when there was no sign of action from the lock I walked down the quay and enquired of one of the other boats what was happening. I was told that the lock had broken down and they hoped it would be functioning again at 12.00 hrs. I reckoned we would have time to take on some fuel too and arranged with the tanker driver to come along to *Liberty* and fill our tanks. In the meantime we had a cup of coffee and settled down to wait. We could see that there were two large peniches in the lock. We saw their silhouettes above us, but still nothing seemed to be happening.

The tanker arrived and we were absorbed in taking on fuel and by the time we were finished we could see that the peniches had disappeared behind the lock gates and shortly afterwards the gates opened. By the time the peniches had exited the lock and the green light had appeared all the boats had untied and headed towards the gates, jockeying for position, but giving precedence to two other commercial peniches.

By 11.45 we were all neatly tied up in the lock like cattle herded into a pen and the gates were closed. In this lock there were floating bollards, and also some fixed bollards. We had a choice and I chose the floating bollards. But a Norwegian boat ahead of us suddenly drifted out into the lock. We thought he must have been transferring his lines between the fixed bollards and failed to get his line on as he did so. He filled and backed for a few moments and then manoeuvred himself in a space against the opposite wall between the two peniches. It is easy to make a mistake when you are not very experienced and we were full of sympathy.

The lock was filling painfully slowly but eventually we reached the top. We then realised what had contributed to the delay. There may have been a need for lock repairs, but now the lockkeeper used his loudspeaker to call someone from every boat to the lockkeeper's office with their ship's papers. The office was in a brick hut up a flight of steps from where the lockkeeper could survey the lock. We had to queue and register our details and pay taxes according to where we were going. We got away with a small amount as we were only passing along the border of Belgium and thence into France. Boats crossing the country to the coast needed to pay more and obtain a licence. But what a lot of fuss for 1.50€ which was all we paid. It all took a long time and it was 12.15 before we were out of the lock, and I was feeling very annoyed with my first taste of Belgian bureaucracy.

Rain threatened as we made our way down the Albert Canal through industrialised Belgium. The contrast with Holland was immediately obvious, and not just because we saw hills for the first time since June. Gone was the pride in keeping everything neat and orderly. The houses were grimy and neglected; industry sprawled and marred the countryside despite efforts to brighten it by adding interesting pieces of sculpture. A sculpture of a man adorned a pill-box on the towpath, made entirely of scrap metal which looked like bits of armaments left over from the war. The Belgians seem to like sculpture and monuments; we had seen several of these sorts of works of art in shop windows in Liège. As we came to the end of the canal there was a huge statue of Albert (a former king of Belgium), and further into the city of Liège more statues adorned the piers of bridges, and in the town we saw more statues and city ornaments.

We turned into the Port des Yachts, a long narrow harbour, in the heart of the city itself. We called the harbourmaster on the radio and he came out to help us into a berth, and asked us to report to the office later. Whilst John tied up the boat I walked down to pay and check the facilities. The port was long and narrow and it seemed a long way. It was very well equipped. There were showers, a washing machine and dryer, computer for Internet, and a restaurant. It was a few days since I had washed any clothes and on my return to the boat I gathered up our laundry. John and I took it down to the office at 17.30. The harbourmaster was not there and I asked the young lady assistant for help as the comprehensive list of instructions provided did not include any information in English.

She did not seem to know how to operate the machine and twiddled all the knobs, eventually persuading the machine to start going round.

John and I then went for a walk into the town. We found a pleasant area of office blocks, a small supermarket where we bought fresh bread, and a lovely park with a small lake and a fountain. By now the sun had come out again and we sat and watched the ducks at the edge of the lake, returning for our laundry at 18.30.

I opened the door of the washing machine to find my washing was still bone dry, and just as dirty. It had been going round in the machine for the last hour with no water! The young assistant must have turned the water off, or failed to turn it on.

We managed to get the water going but now there was a problem because the harbour office was due to close in half an hour. After much discussion it seemed that the only option was to leave it here and return when the office opened again at 08.00 the next day. The young lady promised to switch it on as soon as she came in.

As the office was only open for an hour first thing in the morning there was no lie-in for me next day. I grabbed a quick breakfast and trekked down to the office taking my shower gear with me so that I could occupy my time whilst the machine finished its job. I found that the young lady had not switched on the machine as promised so there would be another delay. I switched it on, feeling a bit aggrieved, but how do you remonstrate with someone without good language skills? I hoped my French would improve once we were spending more time in France.

I next tried the shower. It cost me 1.50€, and I can report that I have had better showers. The main problem was that I had to press a button to get a spurt of not very hot water which lasted about ten seconds, scarcely time to apply the shampoo. I had to repeatedly press the button until I had enough water to have a satisfactory shower.

Back in the office I now turned my attention to the computer. I decided to collect my e-mails rather than trek back to the boat whilst I was waiting for the washing, or so I thought. But no, I would need my mobile phone to register for this particular Internet option. I would receive a text message with a password to use. So I had to go back to the boat after all. It seemed that the visitors' berths were always the furthest away from the offices. I checked the distance by pacing it out and it was ¼ km but it seems longer as I trailed back for my phone. Oh, how I missed my bike.

The Internet worked well and I collected my e-mails in between checking the washing and eventually transferring it to the dryer. By now it was after 09.30 and the Harbourmaster was impatient to close the office. I had to leave my washing in the dryer and I would need to walk down yet again and collect it when they opened again at 15.00 hrs. I would have walked at least a mile by that time, not to mention the miles which John and I walked as we set off to see the city. With such strange opening hours I wondered how anyone managed to get any washing done.

Liège is where the Germanic world ends and the Latin world begins. It is a city that has been fought over for centuries. Once it was part of France as was evidenced by the beautiful French-style buildings with Queen Anne roofs, porticos and pediments. These stood cheek by jowl with ugly modern  glass and concrete neighbours. I imagined these modern buildings had been built to fill the gaps left by war damage. But the architecture was not sympathetic at all and I thought the river front was very ugly in consequence.

Liège is a key industrial centre and was the first city in Europe to mine coal. The roads which were built to transport steel and coal remain but the mining industry has gone, having been replaced by other industries such as armaments and glass. Liège is now the third largest inland port in Europe, after Duisburg and Paris. It is also an important religious centre, having grown from a simple chapel in 558AD to become the seat of the bishopric of the province.

Despite this industrial and religious background Liège is known as the *cité ardente* (the hot blooded city).

We had been given some tourist literature by the harbourmaster, and one of the things we discovered was that the province of Liège abounds in museums. You name it there is a museum for it – cycling, coal mining, glass blowing, pewter making, puppet making, religious art, public transport, paper, pottery, armaments, architecture and beer to mention but a few. There is even a museum devoted to the 'Symbolic Route' retracing, step by step, the terrible route taken by deportees to the Nazi concentration camps. We felt that we would find this too harrowing and decided to visit the Archeoforum, a museum covering 8000 years of history, in the centre of the town. We walked through ancient, narrow streets which in Maastricht would have been clean and bright, and lined with expensive shops. Here they were dirty and neglected, many of the shops standing empty and unused. We eventually came to an open cobbled square, the Place Saint-

Lambert, dominated by a baroque town hall which has retained much of its original furnishings: a double staircase, a lobby with eight marble Doric columns and other ornate features.

To the left of the entrance, a bronze plaque commemorates the most famous citizen of Liège, Georges Simenon, creator of Inspector Maigret. The plaque was put up in memory of the policemen who fell during World War I (the real Arnold Maigret was one such casualty). No. 24 Rue Léopold is the house in which Simenon was born; he was a personal friend of Chief of Police Maigret, and later used him as the model for his fictional inspector.

Simenon spent the first 19 years of his productive life in Liège, where he was born in 1903. "All of the feelings and impressions which we retain in later life have been collected by our 17th or, at the latest, 18th year," he was fond of saying. He began as a reporter for Liège's daily paper and went on to become the most read author in the world, with 500 million copies of his 300 published works having been sold to date.

The museum we were looking for was beneath the square and we descended the steps to the ticket office where we were told by a rather brusque assistant that visitors were only taken round by guided tour and on that day there were two tours, but both were in French. The next English speaking tour would be on Thursday, in two days time. With the rather limited French that I have I did not think we would get our money's worth from a French speaking tour so, disappointed, we made our way back to the river and went in search of a supermarket. We had met a couple on a barge on the river Somme in France the previous year, who had spent a lot of time in Belgium They told us that Belgian supermarkets rival the French in excellence and I had been anticipating seeing the truth of this. We love French supermarkets for the variety and quantity of produce on display. Visiting one was always an event. However the supermarket we were directed to was a Belgian version of a cash-and-carry and whilst it was large and had a wide range of goods it no way measured up to its French counterpart. Disappointed we nevertheless loaded our shopping bags and set off back to *Liberty*.

The day brightened and we enjoyed the sunshine whilst we ate a late lunch and afterwards I made yet another journey to the harbour office for my, by now, dry washing. I was amazed to find that the colours had not run, nor did everything look like creased rags. It had taken a long time and a lot of effort but it was worth it.

Since leaving the Albert Canal north of Liège we had been on the River Meuse which is the major river of western Lorraine, flowing close to the German border. The source of this river is the Langres Plateau in eastern France. In Belgium it had been the Maas, now it had become the Meuse and we would follow it into France.

When we left the next day we were quickly at our first lock. Several boats were waiting, including a small converted tug, *Nomade*, and a Dutch cruiser, *Nerys*, both of whom had been in the harbour with us. There were several peniches also waiting to enter and as we tied ourselves to a high quay, more peniches arrived by the minute. We felt sure that there would not be room for us in the lock together with all these boats and we probably would not get through that day. It seemed that our suspicions were confirmed when the first peniche went in and no other boats were allowed to use the lock with it. If they were going to lock them through one at a time we thought we might as well give up. However when the lock opened the next time, after nearly an hour's wait, someone called to us from one of the other peniches and told us we were to go in the lock with '*Vivacity*'. This was the name of the next peniche in line. The lockkeeper must have been calling us on the radio but we had not understood what he had said. When *Vivacity* set off we followed him and *Nomade* into the lock together with *Nerys*.

Every lock so far had been different. In this lock I was horrified to find that there were no bollards to tie to at our level. The lock was 5.50 metres deep (over 18 ft.), what was I to do with the lines? Ahead of us I saw a woman leaning over the lock's edge, dangling a gigantic fishing line with a hook on the end. The woman on *Nomade* seemed to know what to do and I watched carefully as she looped a line onto the hook which was then taken up around a bollard and passed back to her. Our lines were very short. We now had a long line which we bought in Maasbracht but I had not anticipated using it until we were in France and had not prepared it. When our turn came I passed up the short forward line, which reached to the bollard but not back again. The woman tied it onto the bollard and passed the hook to John at the stern. But by this time one of my bad dreams was coming true, the stern of our boat had drifted away from the wall and was heading towards a work-boat alongside us. The crew of this boat pushed us off and quick-thinking John, tied two lines together, I grabbed the dangling hook with our boat hook and passed it to John who looped his line onto it and once the line was attached he was able to pull the boat in. What a performance, our earlier confidence was perhaps misplaced.

We had to go again to the office with our papers. This time it was just a question of getting a rubber stamp on the paper I already had. In the office I exchanged pleasantries with a young man from *Nerys* and he suggested that in the next lock we should tie to them. This seemed like a good idea and I thanked him. The whole process had taken 1 hour 20 minutes.

We moved out of the lock into a canal lined with heavy industry. We had often wondered what cargoes the peniches carried. Here we saw a peniche being loaded with gypsum from an overhead gantry, and what looked like coarse sand being loaded into another. Further along we saw piles of peat, and something black like coal dust, and later we passed a very dilapidated foundry where we could see a furnace belching its flames into the sky. It all seemed very primitive and unutterably desolate. The smell was nasty too and several dead fish floated by. In spite of this a fisherman was preparing his line on a quayside.

Where was the romantic, castle-filled valley that one might expect to find in this part of the Ardennes?

The next lock was Ampsin Neuville where we arrived at lunchtime and joined the waiting peniches, which included *Vivacity* again, and another registered in Basle called *Rean*. We were ready this time and after *Vivacity* and *Rean* had gone into the lock and moored side by side the small boats hurried in and filled the space behind them. We prepared to tie to *Nerys* but saw that they were struggling with their own lines and were not ready to take ours. Instead we asked the skipper of *Nomade* whether we could tie to him. "By all means" was the reply and we made fast. This lock was one with bollards set into the wall. The skipper of *Nomade* and his partner were doing this very efficiently. They had two lines each so that the boat was always attached by one of them.

When the time came to leave the lock the peniches started their engines and we prepared to cast off and follow them. The skipper of *Nomade* asked if we wanted to go first and I said "yes", whereupon he untied our forward line and cast us off. What neither of us checked was whether John was ready. He was not. He was still in the wheelhouse starting the engine and our stern line was still tied to *Nomade*. The wash from *Vivacity's* engine caused the front of our boat to be thrown across the lock, and I watched impotently as, seemingly in slow motion, we collided with the lock side precisely at the point where there was a gigantic, shining, steel bollard, 'Clunk'. I jumped ashore and fended us off but not before another bit of *Liberty's* paintwork was transferred to the bollard. I held the bows until John had cast off the stern and brought her alongside. I then pushed off and jumped aboard to receive John's wrath, quite rightly, I should not have let the skipper untie the line until I was sure John was ready. More red faces all round.

We were hoping to tie up at Huy one of the oldest cities in Belgium. As we motored into the town we found the old town built around the river, full of character. But the port de plaisance seemed rather small. It also had an extremely narrow entrance, which we would have to negotiate across a very swift current. We decided instead to carry on and tie to a quay which was under the next bridge. When we reached it we found it was fenced off, with metal stakes extending into the river, covered by wire netting. It was obvious that no one wanted us to tie up there. Sadly we decided to press on. Further on we spotted another port de plaisance at Beez, which was not marked on the chart, but the small sign was on the upstream side of the opening and we were past before we realised that it might have been suitable. We were now committed to reaching Namur that day as there were no other moorings before then, and no way that I could persuade John to turn back. This would involve two more locks, but fortunately the countryside was pleasanter, although scattered with derelict-looking small factories, and depressing housing, which presumably had once housed the workers. We travelled beside the railway for quite a lot of the route. The railway and the river hugged the foot of a wooded hillside.

We reached the lock of Andenne-Selles by mid-afternoon, and did not wait too long. *Vivacity* had left us by now and we shared this lock with *Rean*. This time we decided not to rely on anyone else and tied ourselves to the bollard in the wall, transferring our lines without difficulty and after 40 minutes we were on our way again.

Chapter 7 – Travelling On

With Aplomb

There was just one more lock outside Namur. Again it had bollards set in the wall which we managed without difficulty. But the problem this time was the waiting quay. This was merely a concrete wall with holes in and the bollards were set into the holes. The holes were square and large and the bottom edge corresponded with our gunwale exactly at the point at which I had not put a fender – crunch! It was a good job that *Liberty* was a strong steel boat and we were going to re-paint her anyway, weren't we? We knew we would have to now.

It was late afternoon by the time we were out of the lock and motoring to a point where the river Sambre joins the Meuse. The junction was dominated by a huge citadel. The town of Namur was just down the river Sambre a little way to our right and a small port de plaisance was on our left but unsurprisingly was full. More boats lined the quay opposite which was also part of the port. By this time *Nomade* had turned off as they were going down the Sambre across Belgium. *Nerys* was still with us and they tied to a high wall just before the next lock less than 1 km. from the port de plaisance. We followed suit but whereas they went through the lock when it next opened we stayed put and spent the night there. Getting ashore was not easy as it entailed climbing a ladder set into the high wall. Once upon a time I would have jibbed at this ladder, but by now I was quite used to them and I scaled it and went in search of some fresh milk. I crossed the bridge and walked into the little town of Jambes behind the port. I was very tired after such a long and eventful day so was delighted to find on my way a *friterie*, the most popular type of French/Belgian take-away. When I returned to the boat I took with me a bagful of crisp, golden thinly-sliced chips accompanied by chicken snitzels. John was very appreciative.

When some boats left the port de plaisance the next morning we untied and motored across. There were two possible berths. We selected one and motored in to be assisted by two very helpful Belgians from other boats. One even took it upon himself to lower our fenders to pontoon height. Surely the news of our apparent incompetence had not reached here already?

After checking in and using the very welcome and efficient showers we walked into Jambes, and found a delightful French-style street market in process, where we were able to get all our fresh vegetables and salads at a very reasonable price. I added a juicy melon to the load we had to carry back to the boat, but I thought it would be worth it. After a little time in our fridge the slices of cool melon would make a welcome appetiser.

There was a definite French air to this town, even though we were still in Belgium. French was spoken here, and a lot of the food on sale was French – cheese and wine for example, although most of the goods in the supermarket had instructions in French and Dutch. In the supermarket we bought a small shopping trolley for less than 5€. This was a great help for carrying my melon, as well as some heavy goods such as cartons of juice and packs of beer. This was just a modest supermarket. We still had not found one of the truly super supermarkets that we had been told about, and we never did.

At the office that morning I had asked the harbourmaster if there was a chandlery in the town. He asked me what I wanted and I told him I was looking for a large bulbous fender to protect our bows in the locks. He pointed to an opened cardboard box, "I have just taken delivery of these this morning" he said, revealing exactly what I wanted. That afternoon John and I returned to get one, having had it inflated and a piece of rope attached. It cost 75€ (about £50). This was definitely expensive but if it protects poor old *Liberty* it will be worth it.

We became tourists again in Namur. From the port de plaisance there were a couple of small boats which ran a 'water-taxi' service across the river and a short way down the Sambre to Namur, dropping tourists off at various points. It was called the *Namourette*. We took it as far as Namur the next afternoon.

It is said that the name Namur harks back to a legendary dwarf who dwelt on the mountain where the citadel now stands. People came to consult him for advice, and he gave a different answer to each of them. However, following the birth of Christ, the oracle remained mute. Later the city which lay at the mountain's foot was named after the dwarf ("*nain muet*").

History offers a different account. The city was known in the days of the Romans as a point of military significance, due to its strategic position, and at that time it was called *Namurum Castrum*. This is a more likely explanation but I like the first one better.

The Namourette dropped us off on the edge of the Old City, and we walked through narrow streets which were a mixture of town houses and warehouses, towards the main shopping area. The first building of note that we came to was the church of St. Loup. This building had a huge baroque façade and an elaborate tower which dominates the town. The church was built in the 17th century by the Jesuit Huyssens, and no expense was spared. A college was built alongside. I expect at the time they thought the church was wonderful but it was not to our taste and thereafter it was known between us as 'that horrible church'. It was not open to view but at the top of a flight of steps glass doors inside the porch allowed us to view the interior which had a vaulted sandstone ceiling with red-brown columns on black marble bases. It looked colourful but very forbidding.

I found it hard to resist the temptation of delectable hand-made Belgian chocolates on display in numerous shops and had to walk quickly past. But we did stop for a toasted pannini at a small café overlooking the river. When we decided to return to the boat we found that the Namourette was full and rather than wait for another one, which might also be full, we went back on foot, taking the opportunity to cross the river to a small tourist office where we booked for a tour of the citadel next day.

The following morning we drove in the bus up the *route merveilleuse*, a long, winding road that richly deserves its name: virtually every point along it commands a marvellous view of the city or the river. From the top we could see the river stretching for miles in every direction, we could see Jambes and we could see 'that horrible church' dominating the skyline.

There has been a fortress on this site for 8,000 years but there is not much left of the original. Traces of a nomadic encampment have been found dating from 6,000 BC. The first fortifications date from 5th to the 9th centuries, after which it became the home of the Earls of Namur until the 15th century. It was one of the best fortified castles of medieval Europe.

Namur itself continually changed hands until Belgium gained its independence in 1831, and it has been at various times French, Spanish, Austrian and Dutch. It was in use during the Second World War, and afterwards was used until the 1970s for training Belgian commandos. King Leopold II partly demilitarised the site in 1891, and ordered major works to be carried out, including the building of an impressive games stadium which we had passed on the way up and which was being prepared for a circus that evening.

Arriving at the citadel we found a *'petite train'* that was taking tourists around the main features of the site. John was starting to complain of a pain in his calf, and as a concession to this and our advancing age we booked seats on the train and afterwards booked a tour of part of the seven kilometres of underground passages. The train took us to see the moat; the powder magazine (which now houses Belgian film archives – keeps them dry); the draw bridge (which we crossed), the bakery; the forge; and the ventilation shafts of the underground passages as well as giving us a good idea of the layout of the fortress.

Back at our starting point we were taken on a guided tour of just half a kilometre of the subterranean passages. These have been continuously worked on over the centuries and go deep into the hill. The ventilation shafts were added during the last war so that the troops could live down there in gas-proof shelters. Embrasures have been built into the walls where musketeers could fire on approaching enemy. We went up and down staircases and into underground rooms listening to an excellent three-language commentary from a guide with a good sense of humour. At various points he posed problems for the children of the party to solve, e.g. what was the purpose of the groove built into the outer edge of the stairs? Answer: to allow the water to run away. Not so that the Dutch could wheel their bicycles up and down.

The tour finished with a look at a relief map of the citadel site so that we could see where we had been. As we were examining this map the tourist bus arrived and we excused ourselves to catch it. But our guide asked the bus driver to wait a couple of minutes for us. The driver said he was already full so would take his load down and return for us. This was the last bus of the day so that was really helpful especially as when he eventually took us down he detoured and dropped us across the bridge at the port.

Earlier we had noticed, across the river, the statue of a horse which is famous in folklore, Bayard, together with the Four Aymon Brothers. The brothers are said to have lived in the reign of Charlemagne (742-814) who for some reason was angry with one of the brothers, Renaud, and ordered him to be banished, and the horse to be slain by being cast into the river with a millstone around its neck. Bayard survived the ordeal and after many adventures was reunited with the brothers. The horse appears to have had the supernatural ability to adjust his size to his riders and carried all four sons at the same time. Various poems and stories have been written about these Quatre Fils d' Aymon and we found many references to them and their magical horse all the way down the river Meuse.

We had noticed an English flag on another boat the previous day and decided to go along and say Hello. Perhaps this couple would be friendly? They were from the south of England and had just bought their boat to begin their exploration of Europe. They were currently doing a round trip into Belgium and returning to France via the Sambre. We exchanged information with them about possible laying-up places for boats during the winter. They did not invite us aboard their boat but we chatted on the pontoon for a while and they mentioned that they were awaiting the services of an engineer because of a problem with their engine. Seizing the opportunity we asked them to enquire whether the engineer would do a small job for us. When he came to the boat John asked him if he could remove the plug from the top of the port fuel tank. The engineer did not speak English, but with sign language and my bit of French he understood what we wanted and went away to get a suitable spanner. The plug was soon removed and John was delighted. He could now fill this tank, although we still had no opening on the outside to fill it from, and we would have to bring the fuel hose inside the door until such time as John was able to put a filler cap on the side deck.

We filled both fuel tanks with cheap Belgian fuel next morning before tearing ourselves away from Namur. The first lock of the day took half an hour, not bad really, but we arrived at the next lock at 11.00 hrs and were overtaken by a cruise boat which was given precedence and we had to wait until the next lock to go through. Even so it only took ¾ hour. This sounds quick but only by comparison. When travelling through France in the past we had usually estimated 15 minutes for each lock.

South of Namur we finally began to see a picturesque part of Belgium. Limestone cliffs rose on both sides, and attractive towns huddled close to the river, sporting tubs of flowers along the quaysides. The architecture was interesting. The Belgians seem to favour tall houses with hipped roofs, gables and turrets in Gothic style, looking like Noddy houses. There were many new houses built in the old style and old houses which had been extensively modernised. We saw our first Belgian caravan site with little boats tied up along the water's edge. We were now entering the Belgian Ardennes.

Later we passed a beautiful chateau with magnificently laid out formal gardens. I think these may have been the Gardens of Annevoie which were created in the 18th century and are virtually unchanged from the original design. They are the private property of the Montpellier family who are proud to share with visitors their joy at being able to live in such splendid surroundings. Sadly we were not in the frame of mind to stop, and sailed on by.

We had cause to wish that Belgian locks were quicker when we approached the lock at Riviere as it began to rain, heavily, and the rain turned to a hailstorm. As I tied our ropes to the bollards hailstones as large as mothballs were bouncing off the quayside, and thunder rumbled overhead. It only took half an hour but it seemed like an eternity especially as I had to take our papers to be stamped as well. I felt sufficiently confident in the language to say to the lockkeeper. *"Quelle beau temps dans la Belge! Il est comme l'Angleterre."* Yes, the weather did resemble that of England.

The rain eventually eased but we were glad to reach Dinant, a sliver of a town squeezed between the Meuse and steep chalk cliffs. It is a major tourist town where hotel boats and cruise boats ply up and down the river.

Attractive buildings lined each bank and another citadel towers above the cliffs to a height of 100 metres (330 ft.). Most of these buildings have been rebuilt since the last war. Only the citadel and the early Gothic church of Our Lady had been preserved.

The port de plaisance was the town quay where a long pontoon had been laid parallel with the quay and electricity provided for boats, outside several small restaurants whose tables edged the quay and from which smells of grilling fish drifted across.

We were helped in by the crew of another boat who had been with us since Namur and which was moored behind us. Shortly afterwards they untied their lines and moved away. I discovered why when I went ashore. A notice has been fastened to the railings telling boats that it was forbidden to moor there on August 15th – that was the next day. The reason was that a bathtub race was to be held. We decided that we would stay the night but move early the next day. Several other boats were doing the same. The whole town had a very festive air and was buzzing with activity. The trip boats were disgorging passengers who walked along the quay, had a beer at one of the cafes and walked back again. I too went for a walk along the quay and found a small market selling the usual tourist tat – mobile phone covers, jewellery, cheap clothing, etc. Tourists seem to need something to spend their money on. I checked the menus at all of the waterfront cafes and found that the chief item on all the menus was seafood. As an alternative to mussels, or trout, the items were pizzas, lasagne or spaghetti Bolognese. John does not eat sea food since a bout of food poisoning after eating cockles and mussels, and I could not see the point in eating Italian food in Belgium. I also thought the prices were a little on the high side for us, we were not holidaymakers in the strict sense and have to make our money go a little further than the usual two weeks. I decided we would eat on board that night - a fluffy ham and cheese omelette with a green salad and a crusty baguette, one of my specialities. Dinant seemed a lovely town and it would have been fun to stay and take one of the horse-drawn carts we had seen trotting around the town, or take the cable car to the citadel. But we had to go and as we left the next day we saw the bathtubs being prepared for the race, and also another street market being laid along the quay.

There was more paper stamping at the next lock which took an hour, but once through we were again in quite spectacular countryside, dotted with interesting towns and buildings. All that was needed was a little sunshine to make it breathtaking. The journey was dominated by the four locks we had to negotiate. Two of them had no bollards in the wall and the lockkeeper came for our lines. We managed them all with little problem, even though I had to tie two lines together to make one long enough.

We reached the final lock inside the French border at noon. There was a quay just on the border where it would have been possible to fill up with cheap Belgian diesel for the last time. But it was a national holiday and there was no one there to dispense it.

Once into the lock we were finally in France. This was confirmed by the fact that the lockkeeper came to the boat not only to take our lines (on a fishing hook again), but to invite us to come to the office and buy our *vignette* (a licence for cruising the French canals). This was a document which we have to buy every year. The lockkeeper informed me that if I were to buy two *vacance* vignettes for 16 days each, it would be cheaper than to buy a *loisirs* vignette for 30 days. I thanked him and bought my two vignettes.

We still had a vignette bought earlier in the year for *Chefren,* with some time to run on it. I was tempted to use this and decline to buy a new vignette but could not bring myself to cheat. A day or so later I was grateful that I had not done this.

The lockkeeper also gave us a gadget which looked rather like a TV remote control and explained that it was for operating the locks. Great strides have been made in the automation of locks on the busier stretches of the French canals and this was one of the results. We would need to press a button on this *télécommande* at a point on the canal bank where a detector had been sited and the lock operation would start automatically. This promised to be interesting and should speed our progress.

Once through the lock we motored down a small canal with a floodgate at the end back into the main river. There was a derelict looking industrial area here, which presumably was where the slate used to be stored. Black dust covered the ground where a few sad weeds were attempting to re-assert themselves. There were some empty-looking factories and a solitary yacht resting in a boat-cradle not far from the canal. It all looked very bleak.

We tied up at the port de plaisance in Givet. We had finally reached France and believed that we no longer approached each lock with trepidation, but had gained confidence and could even say that we approached the locks with aplomb.

Chapter 8 -: France at Last

Experts?

This part of France, the French Ardennes, has taken some hard knocks. The Germans have invaded three times between 1870 and 1940. But it has picked itself up again and like the rest of France taken advantage of the rebuilding to improve roads and railways.

The first lock was about 1 km. from the border and we saw the radar detector on the bank with a sign saying "Here" in English and in French. Sure enough when we pressed our télécommande the lights became first red and green, then green only, as the gates opened. We negotiated it without problems, feeling much more confident in our handling skills, and pleased with this new automatic system. Once through we motored on to Givet. As we approached a fellow from a neighbouring boat hurried to help us in because there was a strong cross-wind and the pontoons were short and very wobbly. He got a tremendous shock when he grabbed the front rail of the boat, as it came away in his hand. I saw an expression of horror cross his face. The rail was designed to hinge away to allow us to climb off the boat from the bow. He was so relieved to discover that that was meant to happen, and we laughed together as I thanked him.

The small *port de plaisance* provided electricity, showers, and a large ceramic tub in which to wash our laundry with free hot water.

We crossed the bridge to explore the town later that day but everything was still closed for the public holiday. We had a fine view of the town from the bridge and walked down to the quay to inspect a 14th century tower, the Tour Victoire, which was once a castle keep and is now an exhibition centre, closed like everything else.

As at Namur there was a citadel (16th century) which dominates the town, although this was not as large, and another tower (17th century), the Tour de Gregoire, looked down on the town from the opposite bank. In the centre of the old town many of the houses were built of brick and a local blue-grey stone and were very attractive.

The old church was designed by Vauban, Louis XIVs military architect, and its bizarre tower provoked Victor Hugo to comment "the architect took a priest's or a barrister's hat, on this he placed an upturned salad bowl, on the base of the salad bowl he stood a sugar basin, on the sugar basin a bottle, on the bottle a sun partly inserted into the neck and finally on the sun he fixed a cock on a spit".

When we left Givet we entered a lock which led straight into a tunnel. I had been thinking about this tunnel for several days and having a moment or two of anxiety. Tunnels are often dank and smelly places which seem to go on forever. They are usually one-way only; controlled by the lockkeepers or by traffic lights and we had heard of boats which had encountered other boats coming the other way, and which had had to reverse out. We were always wary. But this one was not too long and we were soon into the lock at the other end, Trois Fontaines. The lockkeeper helped us with our lines and asked us if we would be kind enough to deliver a cigarette lighter to the lockkeeper at the next lock, Ham. I wondered if the lighter would spend the rest of the day being shuttled between the locks by helpful boat owners for lockkeepers desperate for a smoke.

It was always reassuring to see lockkeepers and easier when they were there to take our lines. Strictly speaking, the lockkeepers are not obliged to help with the lines but most of them do, and it is customary, even expected, that we should help them with the gates when the lock is manually operated. Whenever we could we would use the winding handle to open one side of the lock gates whilst they did the other. This saves them a long, and often hot, walk from one side of the lock to the other across the lock gates, and also speeds us along. We knew we would not see many lockkeepers for much longer, now that the programme of automation is in progress.

This part of France was the Ardoise, a little finger of land poking up into Belgium and our next stopping place was the delightful town of Fumay. At Fumay the river meanders sluggishly round a bend that is almost an ox-bow, and under a bridge between tree-lined hills, marooning the town on a peninsula. We moored close to several other boats – Dutch, Belgian and German on a newly refurbished quay. A very imposing *hotel de ville* sat by the bridge, demonstrating that this place was the chief town of the canton and has a population of 4475 – how can they be so precise? Surely there have been a few births and deaths recently?

Little electric hire boats complete with canopies puttered by occasionally, and now and then a huge barge would set *Liberty* rocking in its wake.

Dotted along the quay were stone benches situated on a shady green where the local populace exercised their dogs, where children played and where some of the population came to sit, enjoy the sunshine and watch the fishermen. An elderly gentleman walking slowly along the quay stopped to pass the time of day with us and asked us where we were from. That made us feel like a welcome and accepted part of the community. We have met boaters who do not like the fact that the local people and tourists like to wander by the boats and look at them. They say they feel like animals in a zoo. We always enjoy looking at other people's boats and never mind when people want to stop and stare at our boat, and even ask questions.

We left *Liberty* and strolled through ancient streets and alleys which sloped gently away from the river. The houses crowd closely together in terraces along the narrow streets. Some of the houses date back to the 12th century. Once upon a time the town was an important centre for slate mining but the mine closed down in 1971. All that is left is a slate museum in the basement of the Carmelite convent which also houses the tourist office.

We were looking for a public phone box to call home, as we did not have a French mobile yet. The lady at the tourist office directed us up the hill to a small square but there was no box there. We enquired of a householder who told us that there were no phone boxes in the town and she offered to allow us to use her home phone. We thanked her for her kindness but we wanted to make an international call which would have been an imposition, and our call was not urgent. Eventually we were planning to get a French SIM card for our mobile.

It might have been because of the town's location near the border, or perhaps it was just a routine check, but the gendarmes came to inspect the boats. We had first become aware of them when we were going to the office to pay our dues. The gendarmes had been talking to someone on one of the other boats. We had thought maybe there had been a theft or an accident, but no it was an inspection. We were surprised

93

to see that one of the men was very casually dressed in trainers, a T-shirt and very brief shorts. The other three were looking more business-like in normal summer uniform of longer navy shorts and blue shirts with guns at their hips and handcuffs at the back of their belts. Later as I was preparing to settle myself on the deck to re-read one of the few books we had with us I saw them looking closely at *Liberty*, noting our dinghy in davits at the stern and examining our vignette which was stuck in the front window. How relieved I was that I had not succumbed to the temptation to cheat and use *Chefren's* old one. As I stepped out of the door one of them asked me if I spoke French and we continued a conversation in Franglais. Could they see our ship's papers and the receipt for the licence? Next they wanted to know which safety equipment we carried – life jackets, life-ring, fire extinguishers, fire blanket etc. They asked permission to come aboard, and noted that our fire extinguisher was out of date. They admonished us to replace it and buy a second one in accordance with French regulations for this size of boat. Fortunately they took my word that we had life jackets because these were still at home. They were the self-inflating type and we did not think we could bring them on the plane.

Their next request really surprised me – could they see the medical equipment which we carried? I presumed they did not want to see the motley collection of Paracetamols; Mosquito bite antidote; diarrhoea medicine and laxatives that I carried, and presented them instead with my basket of crepe and triangular bandages, burn dressings, Elastoplasts etc. On top of them all was a smart Dutch first aid box, the purpose of most of the contents was a mystery to me, but it looked impressive and they did not even open it – they just marked it off against their list. It could have been empty.

Before leaving, one of the four, who spoke some English, welcomed us to France, told us that the crime rate in France was low but warned us nevertheless to take care of our valuables and our documents, and wished us a safe journey. We all shook hands and they left.

I hoped that they had taken note of our smart little red flag with the white square in the centre which was flying proudly from our jack-staff at the front of the boat. The Navicarte had particularly mentioned this flag and said that every boat navigating in Belgian and northern French waterways must display one. The English people we had met in Namur said they had heard of someone who did not have this flag and who had been sent back by a lockkeeper to get one. We had racked our brains to think how we could get one, and were reluctant to buy one. In our flag locker (a bag at the bottom of a cupboard) we found a flag that the previous owners had obtained for a ceremonial occasion. It was not something we would ever use and it was mainly red and white. So we got to work with scissors, needle and thread and an hour later had a smart flag to fly proudly at our bow.

I had asked the Harbourmaster at Namur why this flag was necessary and he explained that it had come into use when barges were being fitted with engines. Until then the sight of a horse on the towpath was an indication to oncoming traffic that it was towing a barge and they would pull into the side. When the horses were no longer used there was risk of accident as there was no warning, and barges were required to fly the red and white flag at the foremost point of the boat. This makes sense for barges as many of them are very, very long but is an anomaly on small boats like ours, but never mind we have our flag.

We left Fumay early when the morning had not quite decided what kind of weather it would grace us with. There was a lot of cloud but the sky was brighter in the west and one or two patches of blue sky peered out from time to time. Our first lock was just around the bend of the river, and it was automated. Two German boats were ahead of us but there would be room for all of us in the lock – wouldn't there? After all a huge peniche had come out of there the previous day and the three of us together were not as long as the peniche. But either the first boat had not seen us, or was just being bloody-minded as he tied up half way down the lock leaving just enough room for the second boat to tuck in behind. As we approached the second boat made 'back off' gestures and the skipper of the first boat operated the lock mechanism. The gates began to close and we had no option but to reverse back into the river, feeling very aggrieved.

Fortunately the lock operation was quite quick, there was no traffic the other way and we were soon into the lock, which had the lovely name of Roche de l'Uf. It was then that the weather decided we should have rain and we put on the oilskins that we had laid ready – in case. At first the weather could not dim the beauty of the landscape. Thick woods on either side were interspersed with houses. We saw apartments in converted warehouses, and some attractive caravan sites amongst the trees. This would be a wonderful landscape in the autumn.

We had hoped to travel a longer distance on this day, but by lunchtime the rain was sluicing down and we could scarcely see what we were doing. A thick mist descended from the hilltops to almost river level.

We were now on the most dramatic stretch of the Meuse where the river digs its way through tough rock and impressive scenery results. We approached the Rochers des Dames de Meuse, a famous beauty spot. The story goes that three daughters of a local lord, Hodieme, Berthe and Iges, were betrothed to the sons of the lord of Hièrges in the north. When the youths all went off on the Crusades the girls' eyes turned elsewhere – and on the day that Jerusalem was taken were punished for their infidelity by being turned to stone, and now the three rocky outcrops dominate the skyline. I had picnicked here on a previous holiday many years ago and remembered the wonderful view from the rocks across the river valley. Today everything was wreathed in mist and the rain was getting heavier. We motored into Orzy lock and by now water-spouts were pouring off the upper deck and drenching me as I moved about preparing the lines. Water was not draining away fast enough from the side decks and I was paddling, my shoes were filled with water. The only good thing was that it was fairly warm and John and I grinned wetly at each other as we cast off our lines, wiped our glasses, and prepared for the next stretch.

There comes a point when enough is enough. We peered at each other through the rain and said, "Let's shorten today's journey and find somewhere to tie up". John peered at our very damp Navicarte and announced that there was a quay with electricity two kilometres further on. There was no need for discussion, I lowered the fenders and prepared for mooring. Two other boats were moored to the quay already but only a very philanthropic fool would have ventured out to take our lines in that downpour. John brought the boat to a halt alongside the quay, I leapt off and secured our lines, we took another moment to hook up to the electricity and retreated inside to peel off our wet gear and plug in our little electric heater. Soon I was heating hot soup, with bread and paté to follow. By the time coffee had been brewed we were feeling warmer and dryer. The place was called Laifour and we were charged the princely sum of 4€ for the privilege of mooring there. I looked out of the window when I heard the sound of a motor horn and saw a butcher's van delivering to a house near the quay. I rushed out to investigate and was able to get meat for the next three days, as well as chatting briefly, in French, with the lady of the house. I tried some white sausages (*boudin blanc*) wrapped in bacon, with a slice of cheese in the middle. They were so delicious I decided I would later try to make them myself. I believe they are called *cervelas*.

The rain stopped and we travelled on the next day reaching Charleville-Mézières, the gateway to the Ardennes. Charleville-Mézières is actually two towns, the medieval citadel of Mézières which merged with the neat classical town of Charleville as recently as 1966. The town sits on its own contorted loop of the river. A port de plaisance had been constructed off the river, alongside a campsite, but a mistake had been made (or had it?) when building the port and a foot-bridge was put across the entrance with only 3 metres headroom. Perhaps they just did not want big boats in there. We might just have scraped in but chose instead a long pontoon which was on our right as we approached and where bigger boats were tied up

At first it did not appear that there was any room but we saw that a Dutch boat, *Sirius*, on the end was taking up a lot of room and if he moved up we thought we could squeeze on the end. The skipper was on deck and we called to him and asked if it would be possible. He did not acknowledge our request but after a moment we saw him with his wife on the pontoon untying their lines. They moved their boat along with very bad grace and we squeezed on the end, thanking them profusely for being obliging. They scarcely looked at us and acknowledged our thanks with the merest nod of the head. Later we realised why they had been somewhat churlish. Another Dutch boat arrived, there was a shouted conversation and then they rafted alongside *Sirius*. *Sirius* had probably been trying to save space for their friends. The crews of both boats spent the rest of the day in *Sirius's* cockpit.

John and I walked into the town, crossing the campsite whose facilities we shared and passing along the foot of a tree-clad mound grandly named Mont Olympe.

Crossing the river we passed a flamboyant 17th century water-mill. It was now disused and had been turned into an exhibition centre which holds temporary art exhibitions and also hosts the permanent Musée Rimbaud. Rimbaud was a 19th century poet who was born in the town and this mill inspired his greatest poem. He left the town at an early age and did not have any complimentary things to say about his birthplace. But nevertheless the town is very proud of him and had re-named the section of the quay which houses his childhood home the Quai Rimbaud.

We saw the famed Place Ducale which is said to be one of the most beautiful squares in Europe. The buildings facing the square were built in the 17th century of local yellow stone topped by slated mansard roofs (sloping on sides and ends). An elegant colonnade runs around three sides of the cobbled square and an imposing hotel de ville dominates the fourth side. Alongside the hotel de ville is the museum. The square was built by one of the Métezeau brothers, the other brother designed the Place des Vosges in Paris which it rivals in beauty.

The beauty of the square was a little marred on this occasion as there was a street market taking place in it. But it did give us an opportunity to get some farm-fresh fruit and vegetables.

Charleville-Mézières' claim to fame lies in the world of puppets. It was once the home of an amateur puppet theatre, and since 1961 has been staging the three yearly *Festival Mondial des Théatres de Marionettes*, a 10 day event in which puppeteers from all over the globe descend on the town. Courses in the making and performing of puppets are held at the Institute International, in the Place Winston Churchill, immediately to the south of the Place Ducale, and alongside is the Horloge du Grande Marionettiste. On the hour, every hour, this giant automaton pulls the strings for an episode in the saga of the Quatre Fils d'Aymon.

The next day *Sirius* and their friends moved off and we were able to see an Irish flag on a boat ahead. When I set off to buy our daily baguette the skipper of this boat was outside sandpapering a corner of his hull. I stopped to greet him and we exchanged a few words. He explained that they were here for a few days waiting for the delivery of a new SIM card for their mobile phone. They had already been waiting a week. They needed the new card because the phone had dropped out of the skipper's shirt pocket into the canal some days previously. They retrieved the phone but the SIM card was unusable.

We had been planning to move off that morning in search of somewhere to lay up *Liberty* for the winter, this was our next priority. But when I got back to the boat I found

John underneath the floor boards like a mole in a hole, having discovered a leak from the bilge pump hose.

The Irishman, Mike, and his wife, Rosaleen, came round and invited us for coffee and we were able to take a look at their beautiful barge, *Aquarelle*, which Mike had built from scratch. He did not just buy a hull and fit out the interior, but bought sheet steel and constructed the entire hull himself. It was immaculate. I was particularly impressed by the spare cabin which was an office most of the time, but when visitors arrived the table tucked away and a bed unfolded from the wall. It had taken 6 years to build and Mike was still working on it.

They were a lovely couple in their fifties. Mike had a cheerful face with twinkling eyes and rosy cheeks framed by a grey beard. Rosaleen, an ex teacher of French had long dark shoulder length hair and a slim build. Before coming to France they had sailed on the Irish waterways and gave us leaflets extolling their virtues. To reach France they had had *Aquarelle* transported by road and via the cross-channel ferry to Rouen.

They took a keen interest in our problem with the leak. Mike rummaged around in his equipment store and was able to find a short length of hose which fixed our problem. They told us that they were going to an organ concert in Our Lady of Hope Basilica that evening; would we like to go along? It sounded an interesting alternative to watching blurry television or playing computer games and we agreed. The concert was technically brilliant, but rather highbrow. A video camera and screen had been set up so that we could watch the lady organist play and we were able to watch the work that goes into playing an organ piece – the organ stops and the footwork. There was also a Mezzo Soprano who sang several pieces, most of which were unknown to me apart from Rimsky-Korsakov's "The Nightingale". I was also able to take the opportunity to admire the interior of the church, the fluted columns, beautiful stained glass and interesting statues.

The concert lasted an hour and a half, which was just long enough. Any longer and I would have been very bored as classical organ music was not my favourite thing. I would much rather have an orchestra.

Afterwards we joined Mike and Rosaleen for a meal at a Thai-Chinese restaurant, which proved to be excellent. We were getting to know them better, finding we had much in common and a similar sense of humour.

Rosaleen's command of the French language proved to be a godsend and we were able to enlist her help to find a winter mooring place for *Liberty*. She telephoned various places in the vicinity to try to find a boat yard which had a crane capable of lifting *Liberty* out of the water. This next winter we would need to repaint the hull underneath, and also fit the log and depth sounder. It was not easy finding somewhere. We also asked at all the English speaking boats along the pontoon and no one could recommend anywhere with a crane, but everyone took an interest in our search and there was much to-ing and fro-ing with guide books and charts. Eventually we found a small yard, which had once been a peniche repair yard, at a place called Pont-a-Bar within a day's journey of this marina. Mike and Rosaleen had passed it on their journey to Charleville-Mézières recently and said it looked suitable. We made arrangements to take *Liberty* there.

That was a load off our minds and now we were in no hurry. We were able to stay a few days and socialise with Mike and Rosaleen, and the other English and Irish boats which suddenly had appeared. At last I was able to exchange some books and stock up with reading matter. Rosaleen was delighted to hear that I write. She had a large collection of books about the French canals and wanted a copy of mine to add to it.

This was the most social contact we had had since leaving Holland and we were so relieved to make their acquaintance. We had been beginning to think that cruising on the French waterways was going to be a lonely business.

Rosaleen told us that the couple on the other Irish boat, and their friends, had suggested another meal out. They had gone into the town and promised to book a table somewhere suitable as there would be twelve of us. This sounded like a good idea and we waited to hear where the meal was to be. The Irish couple did not return to their boat until very late in the afternoon, and were quite merry. I was not surprised to hear that no meal had been booked, but no matter we all set off into the town later and piled into a typical French restaurant where we had a jolly meal, with coffee afterwards on *Aquarelle*.

It was with great reluctance that we decided the time had come to go and find our boat yard and begin the work to lay *Liberty* up for the winter, and we said good bye to all our new found friends.

The journey to Pont-a-Bar was very pleasant. The sun was shining and we journeyed along the river Meuse enjoying the countryside and the sweeping vistas of low lying hills. Soon we came to a junction where we turned into the Canal des Ardennes, and shortly afterwards the canal opened out into a wide basin at a corner just before the first lock. Several boats were moored there, most seemed to be on permanent moorings. Perhaps they were owned by local people. The lock was deep but we coped well, I was feeling very proud of the way we were beginning to handle the locks with our new boat. We had become very expert with our catamaran and had felt ashamed of our earlier problems with *Liberty*. But we were getting quite expert now, and loved the new automatic lock system with the télécommande. John had got the hang of the way she manoeuvred, and I had my role with the lines and fenders sorted out so that we did not make any more mistakes. Eventually I would have to take my turn on the helm and become confident in helming, but there would be time for that next year.

Once out of the lock we found a boat hire-base occupying the quay on our right, and the boat yard where we planned to leave *Liberty* was on the left. Unable to find space outside the boat yard we tied up on the right and walked round to the boat yard. This involved walking back along a quay and crossing the bridge. We passed a bar on the corner which described itself, in faded letters on the wall above, as Franco-Belge although we were now several kilometres from the border. We could see where once there had been a skittle alley along the wall fronting the canal. We walked past the few houses which constitute the main part of the village of Pont-a-Bar to the boatyard. The name of the village derives from the name of the river – the River Bar, not the pub on the corner.

One of the partners, Dominique, was sitting at her desk in the office and we introduced ourselves. She called her business partner Bruno who cleared a space on their quay and we moved *Liberty* across. Dominique's husband, Jean-Marie, was fixing a shutter outside the office and he spoke good English. That was helpful as both Dominique and Bruno appeared to speak French with an Ardennes accent which I found difficult to understand. Dominique was an attractive lady in her forties with dyed auburn hair. We later learned that her role was to do the accounts and run the chandlery whilst Bruno was the one who got his hands dirty, literally, and could usually be found in his workshop up to his elbows in grease.

That was when he was not operating the very rusty and creaky crane which would lift *Liberty* out of the water. This crane was out of action just then and Bruno was waiting for repairs. We would have to trust that one day soon it would be repaired and capable of lifting our boat.

Jean-Marie showed us round explaining that they were just beginning to expand the yard and that next year they hoped to have a toilet for boat owners to use. In the meantime there was just one of those hole-in-the-floor toilets so beloved of the French but hated by the English. He also showed us a large hangar where we would be able to leave our car if we were to drive out here.

A small Dutch barge, so full of flowers that it was like a floating garden centre, arrived the next day. Its name was *Dimmis*, and the owners were English - Maureen and Ron. Maureen was another school teacher (a headmistress, no less) who spoke fluent French so we were very glad to have their company and help with translating, as well as more book swaps.

We stayed for a few days packing everything up, and I decided to order a daily baguette from the bar on the corner. The bar is run by an elderly couple; Madame was as thin as a

rake but still very sprightly and smartly dressed. Her husband Claude, stooped and shabbier, was rather deaf. I had ordered the bread from Madame but when I went to collect it next morning it was Claude behind the bar. Several large French workmen were already in there sipping their lunchtime drinks. After I had greeted everyone with *"Bonjour Messieurs-dames"* I asked Claude for my baguette. He turned round and reached for a key from a hook behind him. Noticing my puzzled look he led me to the front door. There he pointed to a door on the side of the building. I thought it must be the bread store so I walked to it and unlocked it. It was the *toilette*! He had misunderstood my French. I collapsed on the toilet in fits of laughter but did not have enough French to explain the mistake. Fortunately when I went back to the bar I found my baguette ready on the counter. Someone must have explained. I paid for the bread and left without looking anyone in the eye, but Claude and I laughed together sheepishly whenever I went to collect my bread after that.

Liberty could not be lifted out before we left for home and Maureen and Ron promised to oversee the lift-out and to re-arrange our solar panels so that they faced the sun. Dominique kindly allowed me to use the computer in her office to book flights home from Paris, and Bruno took us to the train at Charleville-Mézières. I was looking forward to getting home, but even more I was eager to come back the next year and continue our exploration of the French waterways. I wondered where we would go and which places we would visit when we began our exploration of France.